Is There No Other Way?

Is There No Other Way?

EMILY ANN ADAMS

CFI

An imprint of Cedar Fort, Inc.
Springville, Utah

This is not an official publication of The Church of Jesus Christ of Latter-day Saints. The opinions and views expressed herein belong solely to the author and do not necessarily represent the opinions or views of Cedar Fort, Inc. Permission for the use of sources, graphics, and photos is also solely the responsibility of the author.

ISBN 13: 978-1-4621-3865-4

Published by CFI, an imprint of Cedar Fort, Inc.
2373 W. 700 S., Springville, UT, 84663
Distributed by Cedar Fort, Inc., www.cedarfort.com

LIBRARY OF CONGRESS CONTROL NUMBER: 2020946383

Cover design by Shawnda T. Craig
Cover design © 2020 Cedar Fort, Inc.

Printed in the United States of America

10 9 8 7 6 5 4 3 2 1

Printed on acid-free paper

For Aiden. We are still aiming.

CONTENTS

CHAPTER 1: O God, Where Art Thou? 1

CHAPTER 2: Opposition in All Things 11

CHAPTER 3: Universal, Yet Individual 23

CHAPTER 4: The Classroom 33

CHAPTER 5: Why Me? (Phase 1: Victim) 49

CHAPTER 6: Perfected in Him 63

CHAPTER 7: Clean Pain versus Dirty Pain 75

CHAPTER 8: What Now? (Phase 2: Survivor) 89

CHAPTER 9: A Man of Sorrows 101

CHAPTER 10: See That You Are Merciful 113

CHAPTER 11: Now Me (Phase 3: Contributor) 127

CHAPTER 12: He Will Make Her Wilderness like Eden 137

ACKNOWLEDGMENTS 143

ABOUT THE AUTHOR 145

CHAPTER 1

O God, Where Art Thou?

*"O God, where art thou? And where is the
pavilion that covereth thy hiding place?"*

—Doctrine and Covenants 121:1

As soon as the doctor put the wand to my belly, I felt a tremor of intuition in my heart. In the past several months I had been through countless ultrasounds monitoring the twins. This time I labored for breath like a beached whale on the unforgiving hospital bed while my husband, Burke, firmly clasped my trembling hands. We knew what to look for, but the signs of life—the flutter of a palpitating heart, the wiggle of limbs, the flow of blood—just were not there. The white coat remained silent, but we knew.

We all knew.

Finally, after circulating the wand repeatedly in a slow and hope-less march over the bulging landscape of my stretched skin, the doctor cleared his throat and with a fixed stare at the monitor confirmed, "I'm so sorry, but Baby A has no heartbeat."

Sorrow crashed down in a tidal wave of shock and pain, and exploded out of my mouth. I gasped in agony and unleashed torrents of anguished cries; uncontrollable, unfathomable until that moment. "Oh no! Oh no!" I wailed over and over, finding no words to adequately voice the raw emotions shattering the air around us. The medical staff, previously bustling with pre-surgery tasks, now quietly busied themselves with their sterile machinery, averting their eyes from human agony in favor of bright-lit screens humming with pseudo-life.

My brain reeled, searching for order in the midst of the hurricane, for context clues of how one logically responds to tragedies such as these. As a reader, I had vicariously experienced multiple scenes where a protagonist unleashes unearthly wails in their wretchedness, haunting sounds that rise up and envelop souls in the dark cloud of their unrestrained grief. I had read about it, but I had no idea that such sounds truly existed; that primal wails of such ancient origins and earth-rattling chaos could be produced from my being.

As my world erupted in emotional anarchy, my mind raced as I tried to make sense of it all. We had come to the hospital that morning for an emergency C-section to save our struggling Twin A and thereby bring his identical brother, Twin B, into the world prematurely alongside him. The babies' fates were inseparably connected. We had settled on names just hours before: Baby A was Aiden Burke, our "Little Fire" who had clung to life with unshakable tenacity up to this thirty-two-week mark. Baby B was Alan David, our "Little Rock" who had progressed with steady confidence and coaxed his diminutive brother along through the endless weeks of agonizing uncertainty.

We knew these infant warriors intimately—our Fire and Rock—and hungered for their safe arrival. After months of bi-weekly ultrasounds, out-of-state trips for dangerous and innovative inter-uterine laser surgery, steroid shots, monitoring, fasting, praying, and priesthood blessings, all that could possibly be done for our sons in utero had been achieved. The time for a new series of actions was now thrust upon us.

We were supposed to be meeting our sons that morning, delicately touching them in intensive care incubators, sending out reassuring texts to our families. The medical personnel were supposed to assess our little ones and hook them up to wires to measure heartbeats, oxygen to fill lungs, and IVs to pump nutrients. I knew micro-preemies who had been born at twenty-five weeks who were thriving children now. We had weeks—months—on those babies. Had we made the wrong decision? Should we have taken them sooner? When had Aiden gone? Days ago, or just minutes? Maybe even seconds?

In my grief, I wailed within the caverns of my mind, "O God, where art thou?"

* * *

When Aiden passed away, there was no longer a need for surgery to save our struggling baby. We returned home. I ached everywhere; my numb mind, my shocked spirit, my bloated body. In disbelief, I found myself still enormously pregnant, carrying one active twin and another still. I longed to reach within myself, to cradle each of their perfect forms and never let them go. We would simply wait now until my body relinquished them.

Against reason, life continued. Our five-year-old daughter, Daphne, began kindergarten. With labored breaths, I waddled behind as she skipped in eager anticipation to the front door of her new school. I feigned smiles and snapped pictures of her big day. With her sister away at school, twenty-three-month-old Darcie went down for a nap. The house was far too quiet, necessitating hand over mouth to muffle the sobs as I clung to an empty bassinet—the one I had worried wouldn't be big enough for two babies.

I wanted to pray, but in my exhausted state I did not even know what to pray for or how to begin. I wanted answers, yet I knew I already had so many of them. I lingered in a fragile mental state of devastation and peace, seemingly impossible companions. I reminded myself that I knew the plan of salvation was true, that my little family was eternal, and I would see my Aiden again. Yet, the tears continued to course. I scolded myself internally. Didn't I know that God had a plan? That everything works together for our good?

My head throbbed as the tears persisted, flowing from red, swollen eyes as if from an endless river of misery. I told myself that I shouldn't feel this way. If my faith were stronger, I wouldn't long for my bed to fold in on me, dragging me into a cocoon of darkness where I could hide away and sleep for years, erasing this all-consuming wound in my chest.

Faith and doubt wrestled relentlessly, leaving me numb inside. I sat propped in bed, staring through my window without seeing. My brain circled the foundational beliefs of my life, inspecting for weakness, checking for cracks. The precious hour of silence that nap-time and school-time afforded me slipped away in a steady march of heartless ticks and tocks echoing in the stillness.

A knock sounded at the front door, jarring and unwelcome. I struggled to swing my legs around and pull my heavy belly upright, hesitant to open the door and interact with the outside world. I had always been a wide-open door, wide-open arms, wide-open heart kind of woman, but today I approached the door slowly with growing trepidation. I half-hoped the individual would vanish into thin air to save me from the draining effort that politeness now required of me. Hiding the excruciating sorrow wracking my mind, spirit, and body felt nigh impossible. But courtesy was ingrained too deep. Against my will, I steeled my heart and twisted the knob with caution.

There stood my neighbor, Arlene Ball, purple bubble bath in one hand and a shiny bag of Lindor chocolates in the other. She didn't say a word, just simply pulled me into a hug. So much for a steeled heart. My ill-constructed dam broke in an instant and I wept with abandon. I was embarrassed to cry in front of her. Here was a woman who embodied Nietzsche's worn-out cliché, "What doesn't kill you makes you stronger." She was a sixty-five-year-old, glasses balanced near the tip of the nose, five-foot-nothing warrior. Every imaginable trial clouded her life: multiple forms of abuse and dysfunction in her childhood, the loss of both husband and child in a terrible drowning accident, the suicide of her adult son, chronic pain, and a daughter facing extreme health challenges. My pain paled in comparison. How could I possibly mourn over my seemingly small loss in front of such a battle-hardened gladiator?

"Oh, Arlene," I blubbered, "I'm so sorry to cry in front of you. I know you have experienced far more than I could ever imagine."

Arlene shook her head and chastised with gentle firmness, "Don't compare grief, Emily. I have no doubt that the agony you are experiencing now is every bit as real and as challenging for you as my trials have been for me. You feel what you need to feel."

With those wise words, I experienced one of the most distinct and mind-altering paradigm shifts of my life as I realized this profound truth: there are no yardsticks to measure pain. There is no score system or balance sheet that says one's loss is greater or less than another's. A miscarriage at six weeks could be just as earth-shattering for a mother as a stillborn baby carried full-term. A gut-wrenching divorce could be as life-altering as a diagnosis of multiple sclerosis. There is no need to stack our pain in competition with another. The various challenges of our lives have the potential to teach us the unique lessons we each need to learn. Our job is to love each other through them, not add layers of pain by comparing tragedies under a microscope, judging and awarding out medals for "Worst Tragedy" or "Greatest Anguish Suffered." We are allowed to feel what we need to feel simply because all emotions, from the elation of pure joy to the depths of despair, are *all* a part of this mortal experience.

I hadn't known I was looking for permission to grieve, but perhaps Arlene did. This woman had been to hell and back multiple times, and yet here she was still turning her wounds into wisdom to bless others who suffered. When Arlene left that day, soul-searching questions filled my mind. Was it possible to admit my sorrow-fed doubts, but not falter in my testimony? Could I embrace my grief and not be faithless? Could I learn to give others the gift of compassion and words of healing as Arlene had done for me? The answers, of course, were yes. I could, and I would.

Though still wracked with sorrow, I knew these undeniable truths remained: forever families, priesthood power, and Jesus Christ's immutable, everlasting Atonement. As I leaned into these certainties, the pain didn't diminish immediately, but my resolve to remain faithful solidified, making breath and speech possible when I was sure I had lost all ability to communicate. I turned my aching heart toward Him, the only One who I knew could truly understand what I was feeling. I found comfort in the words of Sister Chieko N. Okazaki when she explained the following:

> We know that Jesus experienced the totality of mortal existence in Gethsemane. It is our faith that He experienced everything—absolutely everything. Sometimes we don't think through the implication of that belief. We talk in great generalities about the sins of all humankind, about the suffering of the entire human family. But we don't experience pain in generalities. We experience it individually.
>
> That means He knows what it felt like when your mother died of cancer—how it was for your mother, how it still is for you. He knows what it felt like to lose the student body election. He knows that moment when the brakes locked and the car started to skid. He experienced the slave ship sailing from Ghana toward Virginia. He experienced the gas chambers at Dachau. He experienced Napalm in Vietnam. He knows about drug addiction and alcoholism.

Let me go further. There is nothing you have experienced . . . that He does not also know and recognize. He understands about rape and infertility and abortion. His last recorded words to his disciples were, "And lo, I am with you always, even unto the end of the world." He understands your mother-pain when your five-year-old leaves for kindergarten, when a bully picks on your fifth-grader, when your daughter calls to say that the new baby has Down Syndrome. He knows your mother-rage when a trusted babysitter sexually abuses your two-year-old, when someone gives your thirteen-year-old drugs, when someone seduces your seventeen-year-old. He knows the pain you live with when you come home to a quiet apartment where the only children are visitors, when you hear that your former husband and his new wife were sealed in the temple last week, when your fiftieth wedding anniversary rolls around and your husband has been dead for two years. He knows all that. He's been there. He's been lower than all that. He's not waiting for us to be perfect. Perfect people don't need a Savior. He came to save his people in their imperfections. He is the Lord of the living, and the living make mistakes. He's not embarrassed by us, angry at us, or shocked. He wants us in our brokenness, in our unhappiness in our guilt and in our grief.[1]

If what Sister Okazaki said was true, was it possible that the Lord knew intimately and entirely the pain of having a stillborn baby? Was it possible that this experience could teach me to not only rely fully upon the Savior's ability to heal, but that it could also teach me to come to know Him—really *know* Him?

After I lost Aiden, it was as though a film had been removed from my eyes. The entire world had changed in a drastic and irrevocable fashion. Colors, though bright, seemed to display the nuanced shadows that undulated and changed with each cloud that passed. More than landscapes and sky, I found that faces had taken on a whole new dimension. Pain. It was etched everywhere. Why hadn't I seen it so clearly before?

Consumed with this concept of sorrow and its powerful ability to sculpt our souls, I began looking for literature that addressed the topic of grief from a faith-based perspective, specifically told from the viewpoint of women. To my surprise, the pickings were slim and left me hungering for more. I broadened my search parameters but still found myself longing for a particular angle, namely women who had experienced heartbreak, who had remained true to their faith despite their pain and had become better because of it. It was as if I wanted these women's voices there beside me, holding my hand through those early excruciating days, showing me the light at the end of the tunnel.

More than a year later, I realized I needed to create the content I sought for further healing, in hopes that perhaps just one woman suffering as I had might feel my hand in hers, that she might not feel so alone. I recalled Eric Richard's motivational words, "God can use your greatest pain as the launching point for your greatest success." Though I would need months and years to continue working through my grief, I began to foster a hope that perhaps our Aiden had come and gone so quickly not just to change me but to touch others' lives as well.

As I pondered this possibility, a project was born within me as I realized the stories, hope, and inspiration I sought for in literature actually existed in reality all around me. I reflected on Arlene and the others who had come to see me after our loss. Women who had shared stories of their own, who had lent me their strength and wisdom when I needed it the most, quietly emerged from the periphery of my life. I dialed in on their hidden sorrows, astounded again and again by their examples of fortitude and faith despite the trials they had encountered.

I began to make a list of the women, specifically in my ward boundaries, with whom I felt I had at least a basic relationship. They were a diverse mixture on the continuum of faith, life experiences, and personalities. I began to type the names of each of these women living within less than a five-mile-radius of one another. House by house, I recalled their stories. I remembered snippets they shared in comments during Relief Society lessons, testimonies borne over the pulpit and in my living room, service rendered, and sermons given in and out of chapel walls. I wrote their names and the monsters they faced:

Lacie: death of two premature babies.
Donna: infertility, cancer.
Camille: son with drug addiction.
Amberlee: anxiety, OCD, miscarriage.
Dayna: death of husband to cancer, death of daughter to a car accident, blended family.
Charlotte: marital infidelity and subsequent separation.

On and on, I surveyed each neighborhood, the most intense life problems imaginable jumping off the page with words such as suicide, eating disorder, death, depression, infidelity, bankruptcy, chronic illness, addiction. Every household had seen its challenges. Of those I thought had no trials, I quickly realized it was not because the family had no heartaches, but rather that I did not know them well enough to have them confide in me the Goliaths of their souls.

My initial list consisted of fifty women with a range of troubles sitting like sleeping dragons next to their names. At the time, this number represented nearly half of the adult women in our ward. It startled me to realize that if I was sitting in my home hurting from the wounds of my dragon battle, then chances were, the woman in the home next to me was suffering from her conflict as well.

And the next home.

And the next.

It didn't seem right for us to sit in isolation, nursing our wounded hearts alone, rather than offering the healing balm of compassion to each other to vanquish the monstrous influence of our trials together. I knew there was power in connection. I desperately wanted to put an end to the pattern of suffering in the darkness of seclusion and emerge instead into the light of community and sisterhood.

In a bold and presumptuous move, I began to reach out to them. I asked these women one by one if they would be willing to share their story with me and, perhaps, with the world. To my great surprise, they were not only willing but eager to share. Many were ready to stop hiding their injuries, ready to own them and spread the lessons they had learned so that others facing similar struggles wouldn't feel so alone in their struggle. They wanted to contribute, to give back, to spare others the minutes or even years of excess suffering. Fifty women were plagued with pain, yet despite it all, they still showed up—for me, for you, for themselves, and for God.

One of the women I first approached about the project listened to my general idea with a critical ear and then questioned, "Well, are you just trying to make people sad?" I reassured her that while the stories would be honest and perhaps raw, my aim was not to depress but to uplift with four overarching goals:

1. To help those who pick up this book know that they are not alone.
2. To encourage less judgment in our families, congregations, communities, and world.

3. To echo the call originating from our Savior to bear one another's burdens.
4. To realize we can shape our greatest pains into our greatest opportunities for contribution.

As we seek to alleviate suffering in others, our pain gains purpose and utility. Suffering may be a universal concept, but it is an individual reality.

As I studied the grieving process and interviewed each woman, I began to notice patterns in their mindsets toward their trials and developed a theory I like to term the "Growth Through Grief Model." I identified three primary stages an individual identifies with as a result of suffering: Victim, Survivor, and Contributor.

We begin first with victimhood, a space where grieving is at its height. Victims generally feel compelled to ask questions and may feel like they are not themselves initially. Next, we move into a survivor space. Looking back at their trials as if in a rear-view mirror, a survivor is able to gain a level of objectivity. In this phase an individual is able to identify lessons they have learned from their challenge and (potentially) ways they have grown because of it. The final stage is a graduation to contributor. This is where we are able to feel a sense of acceptance and, ideally, peace about our experiences. In contribution we reflect on the ways we have changed because of our sorrows (hopefully for the better). In this final stage, we generally have a desire to turn outward and bless others due to the wisdom we have gained.

Acceptance and contribution are worthy goals, and while one would hope to remain in the phase of contributor forever, the reality is that we often cycle back through these mindsets persistently working toward the ideal of reaching a place of continual peace.

In the following chapters, I highlight brief examples from the lives of each of the women I had the privilege of interviewing to demonstrate various aspects of this Growth Through Grief Model. These vignettes do not do justice to the depth of their suffering or the height of their accomplishments, but are a simple nod to their sorrows and successes. Overall, this book is a tapestry of life, woven from the individual strands of these fifty women. I honor them for their courage to lay bare their wounded, scarred, and broken hearts—the sorrows you may not have seen on Sunday—with the hope that the Healer of us all will one day make us whole again, not just during a one-hour sacrament meeting, but for all eternity.

ENDNOTE

1. Chieko N. Okazaki, *Lighten Up!* (Salt Lake City: Deseret Book, 1993), 174.

CHAPTER 2

Opposition in All Things

*"For it must needs be, that there is an opposition
in all things. If not so . . . righteousness could
not be brought to pass, neither wickedness,
neither holiness nor misery, neither good
nor bad. Wherefore, all things must needs
be a compound in one."*

—2 Nephi 2:11

There once was a woman who had only one precious son. The boy was everything to his mother; the sunshine, music, and joy of her life. Unexpectedly, the formerly vivacious child was struck with a grave illness and swiftly died. In shock, his bereaved mother was unwilling to accept his sudden death. In a frenzy, she carried his limp, lifeless body to her neighbors, begging them for medicine to heal him. The people pitied her for her loss and worried that her mind had been addled by his passing. They gently attempted to persuade her that her son was truly gone, but with each venture she only grew more insistent that he could still be saved.

Resolute, the mother continued to carry his cold form, desperately rushing through the village as she sought for help. At last she met a man who compassionately placated her longings. "I cannot give you the medicine to right this," he said with a sad shake of his head, "but I know one who can."

The man took her to a renowned teacher. Kneeling before him, the woman prostrated herself on the ground, pleading mightily with the teacher to heal her son. Pondering her request, the teacher paused for a brief moment. At last he nodded. "I will do all that can be done for you. However, before I can help, you must first bring me a mustard seed."

Surprised, the woman asked, "Just a mustard seed?"

"Yes, just one mustard seed," the teacher replied. "But the seed must come from a house that has never known sorrow, trouble, or suffering."

Filled with renewed hope, the woman left the body in care of the teacher and returned speedily to her village, searching for the home without sorrow. At the first house she inquired at, she found that, like herself, the family had recently mourned the loss of a beloved member of their circle. Quickly, she expressed condolences and moved along to the next structure. A child with a missing leg answered the door. Swallowing her request, the woman turned to another doorstep, where intense poverty was evident. House by house she scurried, a growing sense of alarm building within. Though the woman found many throughout the village who were willing to share a mustard seed, to her dismay, not a single home had been untouched by heartache.

As the day became evening and then faded into night, the woman slowed her search. Staring up into the star-spattered sky, the enormity of the fruitless task dawned, and she was struck at once with the stark reality of universal suffering. As new understanding converged, her panic was calmed, and she was able to accept the reality of her son's death.

With heavy, exhausted steps, the woman returned to the teacher a changed soul. Extending her cupped hands out to him, she bowed her head in resignation as he surveyed the offering of empty palms.

* * *

This parable of the bereaved mother and the mustard seed, drawn from ancient Buddhist teachings, illuminates the reality that all mankind must experience suffering in mortality. Like the mother in the story, I too was blind to the vastness of human agony until I experienced our own deep loss. However, unlike this illustration, I did not immediately possess the ability to look beyond the enormity of our heartbreak and see it in others. That ability took time to develop. Often, we are so battered and broken from our battles, we must first care for our own wounds before it is even a possibility to take notice of, or assist in, the crusade others are waging. The women who shared their stories with me were not unlike the woman in the parable. Each had to confront the chaos of their trauma before they could begin to sort through and make sense of it. Each had to sit with the pain of their challenges before healing was even a possibility.

Riley

The squeak of sneakers echoed in the gym at Parowan High as the girls' volleyball team attacked their workout with vigor. Riley was used to dominating practice no matter what season and the corresponding sport she found herself in. Competitive in basketball, softball, and volleyball, Riley was an asset regardless of the uniform she donned. She was just as hard-working at home in a pair of jeans and a T-shirt while laboring on the family farm. Young and strong, she was used to feeling the burn in her lungs during conditioning, to muscles straining while hefting sprinkler pipes, to pushing her body to its limits and beyond. There was such satisfaction in knowing she had left it all out on the court or in the field; that she had given her all mentally and physically.

But lately, something had felt off. It had begun with soreness when she woke in the mornings and had progressed to a persistent aching, raging throughout her entire body, targeted specifically in her joints. Today, the pain seared in her back, forcing her to double over, grimacing in misery. The coach took notice and insisted she call it quits, a concept of which this tenacious farm girl knew little.

It would take more than a year before the debilitating pain would be diagnosed. When the doctor spoke the words "rheumatoid arthritis," Riley was confused. Arthritis was a disease for hobbled grandmothers with gnarled shaking hands. Arthritis was not meant for a teenage girl with so much life ahead of her.

Dominique

Dominique's fiancé had shown up on her doorstep, eyes frenzied and darting the morning before their marriage, the distinct smell of sickly

13

sweet weed permeating his clothing. Apologies and promises were pasted over the residual wound of his drug addiction like a thin Band-aid clumsily applied to stem the flow of a sliced artery. It would never hold.

She had always planned on a temple marriage and a forever family. Her journals consistently attested to the hopeful goal she had made many years before. But small, incremental choices had led them down a different path until that dream faded away, along with her innocence. Her ability to trust him was completely destroyed, yet so much time and energy had been poured into their years-long relationship that it felt impossible to turn back. Neither seemed able to admit that there had been too many wounds for their marriage to last.

When the divorce was finalized less than two years later, Dominique was sick with regret. She wondered how different her life would look if she had stayed true to the goals she had made so many years ago.

Donna

It wasn't a possibility anymore, so why did it matter anyway? Removing worn-out women's parts that had never functioned properly, that had failed her and all three husbands, was nothing to weep over. Surgery would mean beating cancer—for now. So why did it feel like shadows of little hands reached out to her and whispers of "Mama" echoed in her ears as Donna signed away her last hope for motherhood, grief aching in her fingertips?

Amberlee

The smell of leather cleaner filled the pristine SUV as Amberlee sped down the freeway. Beside her, her mother chatted away cheerfully, reaching back from time to time to help her two young granddaughters in their car seats.

Amberlee could hardly hear the words. Her obsessive-compulsive disorder raged within, demanding compliance. It was so dirty. Her car was unfathomably dirty. A smudge on the dashboard screamed for attention. A stray hair clung to the console. A rogue blade of grass littered the floor. Amberlee fumbled for the baby wipes, desperately pulling a cloth free and reaching for the insulting smudge.

Suddenly, the car veered onto the rumble strip, startling all four passengers with jarring bumps. "Amberlee!" her mother yelled out in fear.

Amberlee yanked the vehicle back into place, attention on the road momentarily, but her eyes darted back to the smug little smudge that seemed to laugh at her. Her mother reached for the wipe, searching for the nearly imperceptible mark and the right words.

"Amberlee, honey. I think it's time you got some help."

Joy

The hand topped out, pointing to the highest number on the scale. It seemed as though the entire machine strained under the pressure. Five hundred pounds. No, more. Five hundred was where the scale's numbers ended, but not the weight. Joy wanted to cover her eyes in disbelief, to will back the pounds and the shame. Inside, a teenage girl echoed from decades away, "This is not who I am!"

* * *

When a mother cradles the orb of her pregnant belly and dreams of all that the bright future holds for her precious child, she may never imagine the grueling gauntlet of fiery trials that same child will inevitably encounter one day. As expectant mothers, we are providing a sacred space to grow remarkable bodies, the physical tabernacles of majestic, eternal spirits. We may imagine those bodies and spirits knit together in the womb, entering this world in tandem as healthy infants who develop into happy, talented children, and then grow into wise, kind-hearted, hard-working adults.

But the hard truth is, our lives never progress in such a straightforward, idealistic manner. The reality remains, that this life is a struggle. It is growth. From the moment we take our first breath to the second we take our last, our lives are a tangle of conflicting experiences: highs and lows, trials and triumphs. The Book of Mormon teaches, "For it must needs be, that there is an opposition in all things. If not so, righteousness could not be brought to pass, neither wickedness, neither holiness nor misery, neither good nor bad. Wherefore all things must needs be a compound in one" (2 Nephi 2:11).

This compounding, a mixture of seemingly opposite experiences, was demonstrated on a global scale in 2018. A photo of the incredibly moving statue *Melancholy*, created by the Romanian

Melancholy by Albert György. Used with permission.

sculptor Albert György, was posted by an admirer on Facebook. The larger-than-life statue (on display in Geneva, Switzerland) depicts a figure made of copper sitting slumped over on a bench, with a giant, aching hole in his chest—a representation of the void that grief leaves within us. In just nine months, more than twenty-four million people viewed the photo, producing more than two hundred thousand shares, and at least four million comments. These comments are heartbreakingly raw and show the power of love mingled with sorrow. A beautiful, worldwide community blossomed online as scores of strangers united to share their experiences with sadness and expressed sympathy to one another.

One critic, commenting on the artist's body of work shared, "In its complexity and diversity, the visionary art of Albert György testifies to a personal dialectic between suffering and happiness."[1] That personal knowledge was gained from the loss of his wife and the tremendous emptiness that overwhelmed him after her passing. In order to create such a moving piece that superseded culture, language, gender, and age, György had to understand the transcendent power of both love and grief—inextricable companions.

For many years, I was unaware of this irrevocable law, namely that human growth relies on the relationship between inseparable opposites: joy and sorrow, health and sickness, light and darkness. If left without their counter companion, these lone concepts lose much of their significance in the human experience. Does a child born into wealth comprehend the affliction of poverty? Can we appreciate a full stomach if we have never known the awful ache of hunger? Or the warmth of a smile without first the coldness of a frown? How can we fully understand the thrill of success if we have never known the dejection of failure?

As a youth, I naively believed that being a member of The Church of Jesus Christ of Latter-Day Saints meant I would be immune to suffering. Never mind that I was raised on the stories of stalwart pioneer ancestors persevering through afflictions of every kind to both body and spirit. Somehow, I misunderstood, glazing over the trials while only hearing the triumphs. To me, faith equaled armor. Missionaries were always happy and successful. Couples sealed in the temple were always eternally committed. Prayers were always answered directly. Testimony, combined with earnestly trying to keep the commandments, was the bulletproof vest to ward off Satan, sin, and sorrow.

In a talk given at a BYU women's conference, Sheri Dew opposed this misunderstanding and taught, "Lucifer whispers that life's not fair and that if the gospel were true, we would never have problems or disappointments. . . . The gospel isn't a guarantee against tribulation. That would be like a test with no questions. Rather, the gospel is a guide for maneuvering through the challenges of life with a sense of purpose and direction."[2]

Being an ardent follower of Jesus Christ is not a fail-safe from adversity. In fact, history is riddled with examples of believers who were ridiculed, persecuted, and even martyred *because* of their commitment to God.

I distinctly remember the first time it clicked in my mind that many of our pioneer ancestors faced immense challenges despite their tremendous faith. I was fourteen years old, attending a stake-wide youth conference at Martin's Cove in Wyoming, where we reenacted a pioneer handcart trek. Each attendant wore a lanyard around their neck with the name of an actual pioneer and a brief biography on the back. I don't recall the name of my pioneer, but I do remember she came from a wealthy family in England, gave up all her earthly possessions and the love of her family to join with the Saints, immigrated to America, and made the arduous journey west across the plains to Zion.

As we trekked along the sweltering sandy trail, our bonnets doing little to shade our sweaty faces, the physical demands on these early Saints began to become a reality to me. I imagined *my* pioneer and wondered if this wealthy English girl was familiar with blisters and dehydration before her journey began. I wondered if the aching in her back was dulled by the aching of her heart, as she mourned the loss of family and country. I pondered if I would have had the courage to abandon all for the gospel of Jesus Christ when the stakes were so high.

As the heat and the dust billowed around, and through us, I was relieved when our leaders led us into a shaded cove. We sat on a slope in half-circle rows, drawing long gulps from our water bottles while listening to a speaker recount the tenacity of our ancestors who, like the memory of the woman I carried around my neck, willingly forsook all for their faith. He spoke directly about the motivating factors that had propelled the Saints from the Midwest and across hundreds of miles of uncharted wilderness. I felt the sting of shock as he recounted horrors of false accusations, sexual assault, the destruction of homes and businesses, abuse, and even murder. All the while, their leader, Joseph Smith, sat in a desolate prison cell, dejected and confused. Was he not the Prophet of the Restoration? Hadn't he been called to this work by God himself? And yet, there he sat, completely helpless and tormented by the injustices being heaped upon the Saints. In this pitiable conflict, Joseph cried out in misery, "O God, where art thou?" (Doctrine and Covenants 121:1).

How could I know as a fourteen-year-old in mock-pioneer garb that by the time I had doubled my age, I would plead with God the same desperate question as did the Prophet Joseph while cradling my stillborn son? It was under the hot summer sun that I was awakened to the truth that life would not always be fair or easy. The road had never been perfectly smooth for saints or sinners, nor would it ever be.

When Joseph cried out to God from the depth of his sorrow in Liberty Jail, the Lord comforted him with these certainties: "And if thou shouldst be cast into the pit, or into the hands of murderers, and the sentence of death passed upon thee; if thou be cast into the deep; if the billowing surge conspire against thee; if fierce winds become thine enemy; if the heavens gather blackness, and all the elements combine to hedge up the way; and above all, if the very jaws of hell shall gape open the mouth wide after thee, **know thou, my son, that all these things shall give thee experience, and shall be for thy good**. . . . Therefore, hold on thy way. . . . Thy days are known and thy years shall not be numbered less; therefore, fear not what man can do, for God shall be with you forever and ever" (Doctrine and Covenants 122:7–9, emphasis added).

A life of ease was never the plan for the Prophet of the Restoration, nor, as we look closely, for the vast majority of God's children. Our Heavenly Father allows unique opportunities and challenges for our individual journey on earth. All of our life experiences (and I mean *all* of them—good, bad, and neutral) are compounded in one another; connected or "mixed together" as part of the larger picture. Each moment of joy and sorrow, once blended, creates a remarkably unique and individualized mortal life. Our time here on Earth has the potential, through the gift of Jesus Christ's Atonement, to exalt us, giving us the tools necessary to progress toward our ultimate goal of becoming like God.

The Book of Mormon shares this goal. As another testament of Jesus Christ, its contents are meant to demonstrate the power of God over the course of several generations of people and, by their examples, to teach us how to draw upon the blessings of His eternal plan of happiness. However, the opening account in the first book of Nephi begins with the introductory paragraph, which includes "the account of their sufferings" and "their sufferings and afflictions in the wilderness." Throughout the book, the words *afflictions, grief, sorrow, mourn, sufferings*, and the phrase "hard things" are mentioned twenty-eight times in fifty-two pages.

By all expectations, this book would detail a miserable people full of despair from the result of their near-constant hardships. Yet, surprisingly Nephi declares in his opening words, "Having seen many afflictions in the course of my days, nevertheless, having been highly favored of the Lord in all my days; yea having a great knowledge of the goodness and mysteries of God" (1 Nephi 1:1). Despite his sufferings, Nephi managed to document the ways he had been "highly favored of the Lord," focusing primarily on his love of God and his testimony of His goodness.

Nephi never shies away from the gritty details of his afflictions, but he is always quick to acknowledge the hand of God preserving and leading them through their trials. He is a shining example of James 1:12, which reads, "Blessed is the man that endureth temptation: for when he is tried, he shall receive the crown of life, which the Lord hath promised them that love him."

When I reflect on my own life, it's as though I am looking at a micro close-up of a high-resolution photo, each mini pixel of blurred color representing a memory or emotion. The variety of light and dark tones are essential to the composition of the photo. If all my pixels shined with bright white lights, there would be no depth or texture to the image. Likewise, if dark grays and blacks washed away all the color, the portrait would be muted, the figure unintelligible. It takes a vast variety of dyed pixels—the bright, the vibrant, the dark, and even the bland—to create a truly meaningful portrait. No two shades, just as no two experiences, are ever the same.

If left to our own devices, we may sometimes wish and opt for the safe colors and the straight lines. We don't often ask for the unexpected curves, bumps, or sporadic splashes of light and darkness. However, it is often those unlikely elements that, when we zoom out from micro to macro and study the big picture of our lives, turn an ordinary blur of pixelated moments into a masterpiece of creation.

President Dallin H. Oaks said, "All of us experience various kinds of opposition that test us. Some of these tests are temptations to sin. Some are mortal challenges apart from personal sin. Some are very great. Some are minor. Some are continuous, and some are mere episodes. None of us are exempt. Opposition permits us to grow toward what our Heavenly Father would have us become."[3]

The mothers of the women described earlier in this chapter—Riley, Dominique, Joy, Amberlee, and Donna—never held their newborn daughters and asked for opposition. They never prayed for Heavenly Father to allow their treasured children to grow up and experience chronic pain, divorce, infertility, mental illness, and emotional wounds resulting in obesity. Their mothers would have never wished those challenges upon them, but the Lord allowed each of these women, and each individual son or daughter who has come to Earth, a "compounding" experience, born from the unique elements of each individual's unparalleled life circumstances.

ENDNOTES

1. Mary Friona-Celani, "A Sculpture That Creates Intense Emotion," *Totallybuffalo.com*, 2018, totallybuffalo.com/a-sculpture-that-creates-intense-emotion/.
2. Sheri L. Dew, "This is a Test. It Is Only a Test," *The Best of Women's Conference: Selected Talks from 25 Years of Women's Conference* (Salt Lake City: Bookcraft, 2000), 134–35.
3. Dallin H. Oaks, "Opposition in All Things," April 2016, churchofjesuschrist.org/study/general-conference/2016/04/opposition-in-all-things?lang=eng.

Virgin Mary and Eve. Crayon and pencil drawing by Sr Grace Remington, OCSO.
©2005, Sisters of the Mississippi Abbey. Used with permission from the artist.

CHAPTER 3

Universal, Yet Individual

"And we will prove them herewith, to see if they will do all things whatsoever the Lord their God shall command them."

—Abraham 3:25

Imagine the Garden of Eden, the most beautiful site on planet Earth. In my mind, I picture a tropical setting of lush green vegetation where produce grows year-round and giant flowers bloom in vibrant rainbow-palette hues. The sun is warm and comforting, but never stifling. A soft wind tickles the leaves of the shade trees. Life in this heaven-on-earth is simple, pure, and perceivably perfect.

I imagine Mother Eve must have been a vision to behold. No mummy tummy or sleep-deprived bags darkening her eyes. No chronic pain, years of back-bending manual labor, or mental illness tampering with her brain. I imagine her exceedingly innocent, as guileless as a wide-eyed baby fawn in a meadow. With no mortal experience but that impeccable garden paradise, how could she be anything but flawless?

How long do you think she lived with Adam in this utopia? Did Heavenly Father walk and talk with our first parents, training them for their earthly season, for eons or just days before the father of lies came to disrupt their euphoria? Had God prepared them for the encounter, or did Satan stalk abruptly into the meadow like a mountain lion, eyeing the fawn with dangerous, calculating eyes?

What would Eve's future have been if she had remained in that static space? Did she feel content in the garden, or did she have a concept of the need for "opposition in all things" in order to help her (and us) progress from temporal probation to exhalation? I have so very many questions for her.

Regardless of her state of mind, as Satan enticed Eve with the fruit, she was presented with an alternative to her peaceful existence—joy and sadness, sickness and health, light and darkness. A small bite. A colossal choice. Wisdom exchanged for innocence. Progression for pain. Mother Eve was the first mortal woman to face such heavy decisions with crucial eternal consequences. Perhaps we cannot relate to her idyllic time in the garden up to this pivotal moment, but who among us has not been faced with a challenge that takes every ounce of our strength to confront? Each of us must make choices that test us to our very core, yet we can take comfort in Elder Jeffery R. Holland's poignant reminder: "When life is hard, remember—we are not the first to ask, 'Is there no other way?'"[1]

The desperation in Eve's question causes a deep ache of sympathy to fill my chest. Oh, the weight of that choice! Though we cannot know at present if she fully comprehended the extent of the travail that lay ahead, I do not believe she was without inspiration. Perhaps with the phantom echoes of innumerable sobs and endless laughter from her future posterity ringing in her ears, Eve opened the door to all human life with four simple, yet courageous words: "Then I will eat."

How I honor both Adam and Eve for their wisdom and bravery. Without a doubt, their suffering was not in vain, lending me faith to know that ours will not be either. Though our first mother walked this earth thousands of years before our time, we can trace the well-established "opposition in all things" pattern that Heavenly Father uses to prove His children. Throughout every book of scripture, from Edenic paradise down through the ages to our modern day, the repetition of sorrow proceeding joy is detailed at length in the lives of individuals, groups, and nations: "Take, my brethren, the prophets, who have spoken in the name of the Lord, for an example of suffering affliction, and of patience. Behold, we count them happy which endure. Ye have heard of the patience of Job, and have seen the end of the Lord; that the Lord is very pitiful, and of tender mercy" (James 5:10–11).

There is not a prophet or woman of faith mentioned in our scriptural cannon who did not experience their own trials. In the Old Testament, Abraham and Sarah moved to a strange land, struggled for decades with infertility, and then were asked to sacrifice their miracle child, Isaac. Jacob mourned for twenty years over the supposed loss of his beloved son Joseph and suffered the near-starvation of his family. Joseph was sold into Egypt by jealous brothers, worked as a slave, was falsely accused and thrown into prison. Moses faced the wrath of Pharaoh and led his people out of bondage only to wander for forty years in the wilderness. Ruth lost her husband, moved to a foreign country, and had to glean cast-off wheat to provide for herself and her mother-in-law, Naomi.

In the New Testament, Mary, the mother of Christ, watched her perfect son's crucifixion before her very eyes. Peter and John were thrown into prison repeatedly and beaten for refusing to be silent about Christ's resurrection. James and Stephen were martyred for their testimonies of Christ. Paul braved three shipwrecks, was bitten by a serpent, stoned, and imprisoned numerous times.

In the Book of Mormon, Nephi's own brothers attempted to take his life several times. Alma was enslaved by Lamanites and watched his wayward son attempt to destroy the church he worked so many years building. Alma the Younger spent decades attempting to right his wrongs, was abused and mocked as a missionary, was thrown into prison, and watched the very people he had converted to the gospel of Christ be burned alive because of their beliefs. Captain Moroni led his people through dangerous and devastating wars. Mormon and his son Moroni watched the entire Nephite civilization decline into depravity until they were destroyed from off the face of the earth.

Joseph Smith was persecuted relentlessly for telling the miraculous story of his encounter with God the Father and Jesus Christ, was brutally tarred and feathered, financially impoverished for the majority of his life, falsely accused, frequently imprisoned, and finally martyred for his testimony. Emma Smith endured the loss of six children, numerous moves and homelessness, and the martyrdom of her beloved husband. The Saints as a body were persecuted, abused, raped, pillaged, driven from their homes, and even killed for their faith.

Our modern-day prophets and apostles are not immune to suffering either. Many have lost loved ones and endured all manner of afflictions to body, mind, and spirit, both personally and within their families. Elder M. Russell Ballard shared, "Life is not simple. It wasn't intended to be. People think the Apostles don't have any trials. We've had our problems and challenges." He went on to detail the tragic loss of two cherished granddaughters and a prized grandson with the concluding thoughts, "I'm not telling you this to have you feel sorry for us. I'm telling you this because everyone will experience some trials or challenges in this life. None of us will escape from having to make decisions on how we will live our lives."[2]

Like the Apostles, the female leadership of The Church of Jesus Christ of Latter-Day Saints has seen more than their fair share of struggles as well. In a recent video published on the Church website entitled "Just Like You" the ten members of the General Relief Society Presidency and Board are shown with captions that give statistics about their lives. The surprising information reveals that six of the women have had financial troubles, four have experienced infertility, six have family members who identify as LGBTQ+, nine have family with addictions, two are battling chronic illness, two have experienced divorce, one is a stepmom, seven have had loved ones incarcerated, one has experienced the death of a spouse, and *all* have been affected by depression or anxiety.[3]

When you look at this extremely condensed listing from Adam and Eve to our present leaders, it is obvious that no one, including these prominent people of faith, have ever been exempt from the afflictions of earth life. Clearly suffering throughout human history has been a universal staple, an essential ingredient to this mortal experience, not an occasional misfortune. This knowledge is not meant to induce fear as we hold our breath, waiting for the next bad thing to happen. Nor is it meant to discredit the nature of our own personal sufferings. Just because *all* will inevitably be faced with sorrow does not mean our challenges are invalid. Instead, this list is meant to remind us that when our trials come, we can decide if and how "we will partake" of the trial Heavenly Father has allowed us to tackle.

Charlotte

Charlotte's home life as a child had been a stormy tempest due to her mother's alcoholism and the terrible sexual and physical abuse she suffered. At just sixteen, she fled her dysfunctional home and ventured out to find happiness on her own. As a young adult, she was introduced to The Church of Jesus Christ of Latter-day Saints in her home country. She was a deep thinker and serious about her study of the scriptures and discussions with the missionaries. It was as if she had been a planet spinning out of orbit and the more she learned, the more she was drawn into the stable gravitational pull of the sunlight of the gospel. Here at last was peace. Here was safety. "The gospel has quite literally been a lifeline for me," Charlotte shared. "It has been my salvation."

Charlotte hoped that once she was baptized and committed to her new religion that she could create a more ideal family life than the one she had been exposed to as a child. When she moved to the United States, met and married Jack, and began to raise her children in the gospel, it felt as though the trials of her past were a far distant nightmare.

As a young mother with three small children and a fourth on the way, the palace of peace Charlotte had built came crumbling down with one catastrophic blow: her husband had an affair. It was not knowledge of the betrayal that cut so deeply, but more so his complete lack of remorse or desire for repentance. With no hope of reconciliation at the time, the couple separated.

However, things had changed for Charlotte since those early childhood years. Because she could not control the decisions or attitude of her husband, Charlotte reached deep into her inner strength and got to work maintaining a home-life for her children that was safe and stable. She played cheerful music to keep their spirits up, encouraged the children to count their blessings, and most important, she relied heavily on the Savior to sustain her through the dark nights of self-doubt and the gut-wrenching duplicity of her husband. When her mind and spirit could not be soothed, Charlotte lost herself in books to escape the pain and disappointments of her life. The realization that life was not always fair, even when we are keeping the commandments and following Christ, was a bitter pill to swallow. The taste of grief hung heavy on the house.

Pat

Pat took pride in the fact that she had always been the "fun mom." She was ready for adventure whenever it came knocking. Raising their six children in the San Diego area of California, Pat and Stu would drive down to the border city of Tijuana, Mexico, each summer and set up a tent on the beach for a week at a time. If Stu had to return to work, he would leave Pat with enough food, take the car back to San Diego for the work week, and return to pick them up on the weekend. Pat wasn't intimidated about being alone or keeping the kids safe. She was self-reliant and creative, completely capable of discovering enjoyment no matter her setting.

The kids were all raised and gone now, but the Morrises continued to seek new horizons as they traveled the world and served missions. One day, Pat noticed an aching in her back. Medication took the edge off, but the pain persisted. This was the beginning of a long and arduous trek across the rocky terrain of chronic illness. What started as back aches compounded with such intense nerve pain in her feet and spine that Pat was often confined to her bed at times, unable to even walk around the block. Countless doctor appointments, treatments, and surgeries were attempted, but the answers were allusive, hazy at best.

"I used to be so independent and strong. It feels as though the core of who I was has been completely stripped away." Tears coursed down Pat's face as she confided her new reality.

"Now I have to rely on my husband for everything. It's so painful to stand, that most days he does all the cooking and cleaning. He is so good to me, so patient. I feel ashamed that he has to do it all himself now, when for so long we were a team. Some days it is so bad, I can't even go in the bathroom without being afraid that I'm going to have another fall. This whole 'enduring to the end' concept is turning out to be way harder than I ever thought it would be."

Mila

Sometimes, our sorrow is not linked to one catastrophic event, but manifests in a perpetual, drawn out aching over the course of a lifetime; almost like the dull throb of a slowly decaying tooth where a wrong bite can cause a flash of sharp pain, reminding us that the issue still hasn't resolved. For Mila, this continual sore is the result of being a casualty of sometimes deliberate but mostly passive racism.

In Brazil, being a person of color is very common, but Mila found that racism was prevalent even in her own diverse community. As a child, bullies began to tease Mila for her "weird hair," mocking her coarse curls. "It was then that I started to realize that I was different because of my race," Mila said. At a young age, she began to feel a sense of self-loathing because of her appearance. As a teenager, Mila tried a variety of products in order to mimic the other girls' straight hair in an attempt to feel more accepted. "Now, as an adult, after putting so many chemicals in my hair over the years, I can no longer get it back to its original curls, and I feel like I have somewhat diminished my heritage by trying to be like others instead of proudly embracing who I am."

Over the years, and especially since immigrating to the United States, Mila has suffered from the alienating effects of racial bias. This prejudice has manifested at times when she has been watched closely at stores to make sure she isn't doing anything suspicious or has had people speak to her in Spanish, even though she is not Hispanic. In the LDS culture, she has sometimes been excluded from groups of women who, perhaps unknowingly, distance themselves from that which is different to them culturally.

Sometimes, people try to draw attention to her race in a way that they intend to be nice, but instead feels like a backhanded slap. Mila explained, "Whenever I'm paid a compliment that is attached to the color of my skin, like, 'You're beautiful, for a black girl,' it's hard for me to hear they don't think that's the norm for my skin tone. I understand that most of the time people are not even aware of the racist undertones, but it hurts to hear the implication that your race diminishes your capacity of being beautiful."

These often subtle comments or behaviors are upsetting, especially when they come from a community that is meant to love and accept others the way that Christ taught. Although Mila has learned to be proud of her Brazilian heritage and dark skin, it is a sad reality that both she and her children will continue to face elements of bias until racial prejudice is eradicated. Until then, Mila has learned to focus on those who see her as a full person and has been grateful for those who have loved and embraced her regardless of their differences.

LaNette

In the space of just three years, the Sowby family suffered more sorrows than most people see in an entire lifetime. Some of their major challenges began with infertility which was followed by the miraculous pregnancy and birth of their micro-preemie daughter at just twenty-five weeks gestation. Their precious baby girl spent ninety-seven exhausting days in the neonatal intensive care unit before graduating to a specialized health regime at home. The daily, suffocating stress of keeping their preemie baby alive and, later, caring for her developmental challenges morphed into further stress from the astronomical medical bills and unexpected job losses.

Unbelievably, those struggles began to feel "easy" when LaNette's dear mother was diagnosed with cancer. During her mother's treatments, LaNette was shocked by the news that she was pregnant yet again. However, another premature delivery did not result in the expected graduation from the NICU. Instead, a level of grief unlike anything they had yet encountered shrouded the entire family as they laid their first precious son, Vaughn, to rest.

Within a year of his devastating death, LaNette's husband, Courtney, was bedridden with an unidentifiable neurological disorder. While they desperately sought for answers and financial assistance for the ever-mounting medical bills, LaNette's mother died unexpectedly and suddenly from the insanely swift return of her cancer. LaNette didn't think it was possible for a human body to survive this level of stress and grief. But the problems weren't over yet. What she and her husband had hoped would be just a temporary illness was eventually diagnosed as multiple sclerosis, the same wretched disease that had eaten away the health of Courtney's father and confined him to a wheelchair. Courtney was unable to work due to the near-constant pain. LaNette began hunting for work while simultaneously searching for treatments to help ease Courtney's chronic suffering when—surprise! Another pregnancy led to the safe arrival of their second son while, at the same time, her father began to have heart failure. It made me shake my head, leaving me tired just from listing it all out, exhausted to think of living it.

LaNette was so steady through it all, but she got to the point where she felt completely numb inside. She didn't have the option of falling apart when so many were counting on her to be the solid rock in the midst of their stormy seas. She played her role, but sometimes she wished she could be the one to fall apart for once. Sometimes she wondered if God was playing some cruel joke on them. Surely, He could not intend for one family to suffer so very much.

* * *

I wonder if Mother Eve could have seen the highs and lows that her posterity would face, if she would have still made the same decision. That one small bite brought about the scriptural promise of compounded joy and pain for all mankind. Charlotte found happiness by embracing the gospel and yet was challenged by the betrayal of her husband's infidelity. Pat had a happy marriage and many vibrant adventures, but her physical pain in her later years left her feeling defeated. Mila felt conflicted with pride and shame induced by unkind mistreatment over her racial heritage. LaNette and her family were drawn close to the Lord through their numerous heartbreaks, but sometimes wondered why God seemed to be disproportionately doling out excessive adversity to what felt like their family alone. Could the heavy challenges each of these women face outweigh the numerous other experiences of their lives—positive, negative, and neutral? Was it "fair" for Adam and Eve to make a decision that would dramatically affect their posterity without our consent?

Rest assured, we signed up for this life. *All* of this life. The delights, the discouragements, the sunrises and sunsets, the mess and the miracle that is mortality! Regardless of whether our first parents' choice was "equitable" as it affected all mankind, we can take comfort in knowing that if we came to Earth, that means we accepted the mixed bag of experiences that would come throughout our probationary state. It was through the gift of agency that each of us chose to follow God's eternal plan of happiness, come what may.

When I interviewed these women, our focus was primarily on their griefs and how they coped with them. However, I could have just as easily interviewed them about their successes and joys. As I reflect on the conversations we had, there were always shared elements of happiness, times of triumph, deep love felt, and important lessons learned, woven through the narrative of sorrow so tightly, one seemed incapable of being extradited from the other.

No, I choose to believe that Eve understood the consequences of her actions. I believe that she had confidence in her children, especially her noble daughters, that they would meet their adversities and rise to face them with courage and resilience, for "men are that they might have joy!" (2 Nephi 2:25). This confidence in the divine wisdom of Mother Eve breathes faith and hope into me as I turn my heart to a God of both justice and mercy, trusting that our sorrows felt in the night will be turned into joy in the morning.

President Russell M. Nelson has said, "The joy we feel has very little to do with the circumstances of our lives and everything to do with the focus of our lives."[4]

No matter the origins of our challenges, we can determine to believe that the way we choose to respond to pain is an essential part of God's plan for our progression. We cannot transition from Eden to eternity without it.

ENDNOTES

1. Jeffrey R. Holland, "The Inconvenient Messiah," *Ensign*, 1982.
2. M. Russell Ballard, Facebook page, facebook.com/mrussell.ballard, July 19, 2017.
3. "Just Like You," churchofjesuschrist.org/media/video/2019-05-1000-just-like-you?lang=eng.
4. Russell M. Nelson, "Joy and Spiritual Survival," churchofjesuschrist.org/study/general-conference/2016/10/joy-and-spiritual-survival?lang=eng, April 2016.

CHAPTER 4

The Classroom

*"Come unto me, all ye that labour and
are heavy laden, and I will give you rest.
Take my yoke upon you, and learn of me;
for I am meek and lowly in heart: and
ye shall find rest unto your souls. For my
yoke is easy, and my burden is light."*

—Matthew 11:28–30

How does pain materialize in each of our lives? What forms can it take? Elder Robert D. Hales described several categories of suffering: suffering that tries and tests us, self-inflicted suffering, suffering to develop our spiritual strength, suffering to humble us and lead us to repentance, suffering from infirmities of our mortal bodies, and suffering from separation by death.[1] I would also add, suffering due to the agency of another.

These categories may seem broad and overgeneralized, perhaps even a bit heartless, until they are given a human face. Exploring sorrow is of little benefit if it is only applied in clinical, general terms. It is when we touch on the reality of their effects on individuals and apply these experiences and lessons learned to our own lives that they gain true value.

The women I had the privilege of interviewing fell into at least one of these categories. Often, they fell into *all* of them. Though they are not prophets with their stories immortalized in scripture, nor Apostles speaking to millions at general conference, each of these women have stories that matter. Just as *your* story, your pain, and your healing are significant. Your stories are important to the people who know and love you but, most important, they are meaningful to our Heavenly Father and His son Jesus Christ. Your trials, and subsequent growth, matter to Him because *you* are of infinite worth to Him. He is there for us through all variations of suffering, ready to offer strength and comfort, healing and hope whenever we turn to Him.

To make a full list of the near-endless ways human beings have suffered since creation would be nigh impossible. Most spirits and minds can only weather a sprinkling of concentrated sorrow, rather than an immersion course. Below are several vignettes, by way of example, taken from the lives of my interviewees to represent Elder Hales' list. These are followed by cases from the scriptures to illustrate the types of suffering that one may encounter upon their life's journey. Though they may seem to be mere droplets when compared to the vast oceans of grief throughout history, the remarkable fact remains that our Savior, Jesus Christ, mercifully redeemed us so that He could understand each heartache intimately and completely.

Suffering That Tries and Tests Us

Annie

They came to her with just the clothes on their back. Annie knew that her niece wasn't doing well, that she had never fully been clean from the drugs that had plagued her life. It had always troubled her to think of those sweet babies being raised by a mother who could barely care for herself. But what could Annie do? They weren't her grandchildren. She knew her sister's cancer kept her hands tied as well. Her health would never allow her to swoop in to raise these two neglected grandbabies, but the guilt Annie felt for doing nothing was eating her away inside.

And then—bam!

They were suddenly there, in her home, part of her family. What was she supposed to do with a busy fifteen-month-old and his seven-year-old sister? It felt like eons since her youngest son, now eight, had needed diaper changes or comfort in the night. Her anxiety soared through the roof. With four children of her own, working part-time, juggling their schedule of soccer, softball, basketball, jobs, stake Young Women's responsibilities, and her husband's elders quorum calling, adding two children with severe emotional issues to the mix felt almost absurd. But how could they possibly turn them away?

When they set up the borrowed crib in the master bedroom, baby Liam smiled as he smashed his head into the bars over and over again. Annie was almost hysterical. She couldn't make him stop. The therapist said babies who have been neglected sometimes do this as a way to self-soothe, to rock themselves to sleep when no arms are there to cradle and caress. It was his deeply ingrained habit now. They cushioned the slats, but each night the rhythmic jarring of his head against bars was enough to make a tough man weep.

His sister, Lila, was vigilant in her care for her brother. It was she who had fed, changed, and entertained the baby when she wasn't at school. She followed Annie around the house like a back-seat driver in mini-mother form. "It's time for his bottle. Did he get his nap? Have you changed his diaper?" It would be months before this little-girl-turned-adult could trust that her new family would meet his needs. Would meet *her* needs. That she could just *play*, be a child, be safe and stable and loved, seemed a reality beyond her mind's ability to grasp.

The dynamic of home changed for Annie's entire family; the original six, as well as the bonus two. Though unforeseen and, perhaps, initially unsettling, the children responded in remarkable ways—all of them. Tonight, her eighteen-year-old was reading to Lila, tucked up under his arm with her favorite story. Liam's baby laughter filled the house as Annie's teenage daughters chased him around the couch, delighted by his perma-grin set in chubby cheeks.

They went to bed happy, the entire busy home. All was still until Annie suddenly smacked her husband's arm in bed and whispered, "Listen!"

"What is it?" he mumbled sleepily.

"No banging," she responded.

Scriptural Accounts

It's surprising how often suffering "to test and try" us is represented in the scriptures. For biblical women in particular, this is played out in examples of barrenness, or what we would term today as infertility. Hannah, Sarah, Rebecca, Rachel, and Elisabeth dealt with the sorrow of being unable to bear children, but eventually they each gave birth to special sons who would mature into men of God. Although the eventual desired blessing was realized for these women in mortality, that does not take away the years of heartache and (for Sarah and Elisabeth) *decades* of what may have felt like unanswered prayers. Hannah, the mother of the prophet Samuel pleaded in bitterness of soul, "O, Lord of hosts . . . look on the affliction of thine handmaid, and remember me" (1 Samuel 1:10–11).

To some, from the outside looking in, our suffering may seem inconsequential. Hannah's husband, Elkanah, though perhaps trying to comfort his wife came across as dismissive of her pain when he asked, "Why weepest thou? And why eatest thou not? And why is thy heart grieved? Am not I better than ten sons?" (1 Samuel 1:8).

You may have experienced this. Sometimes, when a person's sorrow is not obvious to the visible eye, it may be easy for others to overlook just how badly someone is hurting. Several of the women I interviewed, who themselves dealt with infertility, mentioned the misery they felt when other mothers would complain about their children without realizing how desperately these infertile mothers wished they had any child at all.

Perhaps one of the most difficult things about our trials is not so much that we suffer them, but that we must deal with added layers of pain as a result of the actions, words, or judgments of other people on top of it. For these biblical women, the agony of their barrenness was compounded by the social expectations of their day. In their time, it was believed that infertility was a punishment from God and that having children defined the worth and value of a woman.

Sarah (wife of Abraham) and Rachel (wife of Jacob) were both so desperate for their husbands to have posterity that they offered their hand-maids in their place in order to bear children. When Sarah was eventually visited by an angel of God to inform her that she would at last have a child, her reaction was one of disbelieving laughter. She was ninety years old and "the manner of women" (Genesis 18:11) (her menstrual cycle) had stopped long before. How could the promised blessings of the Lord be realized at her age?

How many of us feel we are beyond the point of saving or that the blessings we *should* have received are far behind us? The great hope that these scriptural stories bring us is that although we may be tested to our limits, nothing we endure is beyond the power of our Heavenly Father to make right. As He gently rebuked Sarah, "Is anything too hard for the Lord?" (Genesis 18:14).

No matter how long or hard the road, the Lord will be by our side the entire journey. Despite all doubts, an elderly, barren Sarah became the mother of nations. God's covenants will be made sure.

Self-Inflicted Suffering

Arlene

Forty years. It has been more than forty long years, and she is still angry at God. She had been on the shore that ugly day, looking on in agonizing helplessness as they sunk below the water for the last time. Her precious toddler. Her strong husband. Gone. It was too much to bear their irreplaceable loss. It is still too much. "I still, to this day, feel that sense of disbelief and shock. They are still real to me. Their smiles and bodies and voices."

The decades have brought wisdom, although the pain is still as sharp and real as ever for Arlene. In a moment of introspection, she shared, "One thing I can tell you is that almost all of my life's hardship and tragedy have happened because someone—often me—failed to obey commandments. Had I been in church that fateful day. Had I been sober. Had David been sober. They would still be alive. I do not think my tragedies or hardships were a punishment. But they are consequences. I *do* think God protects others who make bad decisions. I *do* think I got more than my share. But I also clearly recognize that righteousness matters."

Scriptural Accounts

Arlene's forty years of suffering brings to mind the ancient Israelites who wandered for forty long years in the wilderness. The Lord sent Moses to free the children of Israel after centuries of servitude to the Egyptians. Following their miraculous liberation, Moses was instructed to lead the Israelites to the promised land. Sadly, the people were not willing to fully commit to the Lord and instead of going to a land of milk and honey, they were instructed to remain in the wilderness until their hearts were softened and their devotion to God was solidified.

While enduring their wanderings, Miriam, the sister of the prophet Moses, complained against her brother. Miriam was known as a prophetess and in the past she had received the word of the Lord. However, due to pride, she brought self-inflicted suffering upon herself and she was struck with leprosy.

As I think of Miriam and reflect on my own life, I cringe thinking how many times I have endured suffering as a consequence for my mistakes. I can think of one instance in particular where, as a young college student, I was given a clear prompting from the Lord. In my pride and stubbornness, I ignored the warning of the Holy Ghost and, as a result, faced years of residual heartache. The Lord was not "punishing" me for my actions, but I still suffered the natural ramifications for my behavior. Even in the midst of my small rebellion, I knew I could not access His promised blessings without adhering to my end of the bargain.

Mercifully, through the power of Jesus Christ's Atonement and the gift of repentance, our self-inflicted sorrow can be made right: "Though your sins be as scarlet, they shall be as white as snow; though they be red like crimson, they shall be as wool" (Isaiah 1:18).

Suffering to Develop Our Spiritual Strength

Shelley

In some ways, Shelley felt equally as close to her grandmother as she did to her mother. Grandma was an inborn nurturer and had always made space for Shelley in her life, showering her with her time, attention, and affection. It had been far more painful than she had expected to watch Grandma decline from the loving woman who embraced life to the fullest to this nearly empty shell of a body.

It was Shelley's turn to nurture now. After Grandma's stroke left her paralyzed and unable to swallow, her family brought her home and made her as comfortable as possible, knowing her time was soon. Though the days and nights were long, it was a privilege, not a burden, for Shelley to pour her loving service back into the soul that had filled her up with love and encouragement her entire life.

One night, while sleeping in the same room with Grandma to be near if she needed anything, Shelley woke in the middle of the night to the feeling of an amazing presence. Seeing nothing, she closed her eyes and was astounded to see family members around her. "It wasn't like I was imagining it, it was so pure. I mean they were there! I opened my eyes to see them because, you know, that's the natural man in you. I opened my eyes and nobody was there. It wasn't like they were coming to get her. They were just there for her—it was such a testament to me that not only is our Heavenly Father there for us, but literally angels are there. They are around us all the time; we just don't see them! Life gets in the way. It was the first time I realized heaven is right there with us. Our family is *literally* right there with us."

Scriptural Accounts

Abish, a Lamanite convert of surpassing faith, was a servant to the queen of King Lamoni. It must have been an extreme challenge for her to live among her people, knowing that she alone had a testimony of the gospel. When Ammon, a Nephite prince, son to King Mosiah, came to the Lamanites as a humble missionary, I wonder if hope swelled within Abish. Perhaps she wished for an opportunity to speak with him, to assess whether or not he believed as she did. It may be that she yearned for an end to her spiritual isolation.

Once Abish learned that the king, queen, and Ammon had all fallen to the ground unconscious, overcome by the spirit, Abish recognized that the power of God was present and in joyful anticipation she gathered the people to witness the event. With a touch of her hand, Abish raised the queen, who bore testimony of Jesus Christ. Upon raising King Lamoni and Ammon, who also bore powerful witnesses, many Lamanites believed and were converted to the gospel of Christ (see Alma 19:16–36).

Though the Book of Mormon isn't explicit on the effect this miraculous experience had personally upon Abish, it isn't hard to imagine the joy she must have felt to at long last be able to share her testimony openly. These trials that are sent to develop our spiritual strength have the capacity to root our faith deep in gospel soil and produce fruits of the spirit that bring a sweetness and fulness to our lives.

Suffering to Humble Us and
Lead Us to Repentance

Amy

It's amazing how one moment life can feel so right, everything can be going so smoothly, and in a blink it can all fall to pieces. After the unexpected death of her father, Amy knew she wanted to do everything in her power to be with her family eternally. Within a year of his passing, she was overjoyed to enter the temple and receive her endowment. Things felt so peaceful, so balanced in her life, but all too soon temptations rocked her to the core.

Amy explained, "You know, we all have moments of listening to the adversary, every one of us. I went to the temple and was on such a good path. Only two years after that, I was excommunicated, because I listened to the wrong voice. I did some pretty horrible things. I took for granted that I was able to make good choices and started making questionable choices instead. I still struggle with one of the choices that I made. A lot of people let the decisions they make define them and never allow themselves to move past them. I've tried my best to move forward, but I still feel like I haven't fully made amends."

It's not in Amy's nature to give up. Through the power of repentance, she was re-baptized, which has brought her much peace. She is still often unhappy with the consequences that have followed from choices made by listening to the wrong voice. Yet, despite her remorse, she still shows up, still joins a ward family that recognizes church is a hospital for the sick, not a museum for saints. Amy is still found reaching for the Master, the only One with the power to right all wrongs. As she moves forward with faith, she has determined to listen to His voice alone.

Scriptural Accounts

In the Book of Mormon, Sariah, the mother of Nephi and wife to the prophet Lehi, was worried sick about her sons. It had been weeks since her four boys had left their camp in the wilderness and traveled over a hundred miles back to Jerusalem to obtain the brass plates for their father. As the days stretched on, Sariah began to complain against her husband, "telling him that he was a visionary man; saying:

Behold thou hast led us forth from the land of our inheritance, and my sons are no more, and we perish in the wilderness" (1 Nephi 5:2).

In an effort to comfort his wife, Lehi responded, "I know that I am a visionary man; for if I had not seen the things of God in a vision I should not have known the goodness of God" (1 Nephi 5:4). Sariah continued to mourn for her sons, until the joyful day when they returned safely to camp, their mission fulfilled, with the brass plates in hand.

"And she spake, saying: Now I know of a surety that the Lord hath commanded my husband to flee into the wilderness; yea, and I also know of a surety that the Lord hath protected my sons, and delivered them out of the hands of Laban, and given them power whereby they could accomplish the thing which the Lord hath commanded them. . . . And it came to pass that they did rejoice exceedingly, and did offer sacrifice and burnt offerings unto the Lord; and they gave thanks unto the God of Israel" (1 Nephi 5:8).

This stretching experience allowed Sariah to be humbled and to repent of her murmurings, allowing her to draw closer to her husband, to her children, and especially to the Lord. Similar to Self-Inflicted Suffering, these occasions of needful repentance are set apart by a willingness to turn our hearts in meekness back to God when we have gone astray. As we strive to make restitution for our wrongs and remain obedient to God's laws, these lessons can be formative to our spiritual growth.

Suffering from Infirmities of Our Mortal Bodies

Loie and Pete

The horrific crash of metal on asphalt was completely out of sync with the cheerful blue skies on a perfect summer day. Pete remembers feeling the sun on his back, almost *through* his back to the warmth of the road under him where the tires of his convertible had run completely over the top of him, crushing all of his vital organs. They had called his mother and said simply that her sixteen-year-old son had been in a car accident. They didn't tell her he was breaths away from taking his last. They didn't want her to speed to get to her boy before he passed. When she arrived, they confirmed that he probably wouldn't last the night. It was as if his spirit, listening through the drug-induced coma, bowed his back. Pete was never one to step away from a challenge.

Watch me.

They said he would never walk again. Within two years of intense recovery, Pete enlisted in the Marine Corps, determined to hold his own with any obstacle or hard-nosed soldier he encountered. A year into his service, he was still proving his point, when the lasting trauma on his body began to catch up to him.

Loie knew going into their marriage that Pete's health would be a constant issue. But she loved him. She knew what she was signing up for. Or at least, she thought she did. Who can actually know as a twenty-year-old the grueling test perpetual chronic pain would be to all of them, including the yet unborn children that would follow? Surgery after surgery. Debilitating migraines. Abdominal pain that never stopped. Pancreatitis flare-ups that morphine didn't touch. The challenges were often all-consuming.

"There were some periods of improvement, but if I'm being honest, Pete's chronic pain has been a central focus our entire marriage," Loie said. Spreading her arms wide she continued, "We are talking *decades* of suffering. Of course, it's been hard on me and the kids. But what I wouldn't do to take it away from him. To see him without pain—it's almost impossible for me to imagine."

Pete hurt so awful most days that sometimes—often—death was yearned for as a sweet relief. Suicidal thoughts plagued him constantly. "You can't do this anymore," the adversary whispered daily. "You're not strong enough. It's too much for you. Too much for her. You can't possibly get back up again."

Watch me.

Scriptural Accounts

In the scriptures, many stories are told of individuals who suffered from physical infirmities of the mortal body, but as with all of our trials, some allowed their physical challenges to turn them to the Savior, while others did not. In the New Testament we learn of a woman who had an issue of blood for twelve years.

We know from the Bible that, according to the Mosaic law, an open, running sore classified a person as unclean. The law went further to state that anything or anyone that the person touched was also made unclean (see Leviticus 15:2–15, 19–30). We can thereby assume that whatever her specific medical condition may have been, she would have been considered unclean and probably had little contact with other humans, perhaps even her own family. Her existence must have been one of isolation, loneliness, and extreme discouragement after so many years with no relief.

Having "heard of Jesus" (Mark 5:27), she defied the law and went out in the streets, desperate to find the man who could heal her, which in and of itself was an act of faith and hope. When it appeared that the crowd would be too thick to speak with Him, she squeezed through the crowd and, reaching for Him, managed only to touch the hem of His garment. Instantaneously, "she felt in her body that she was healed of that plague" (Mark 5:29) and consequently would be clean according to the Law of Moses. This glorious cure would allow her to be accepted back into the social circles of the day and grant her admission back into the temple. Imagine her relief and the immediate changes in a life that has been fettered by this disease for more than a decade.

Ailments of the body and mind can potentially be all-consuming emotionally, mentally, and physically. When it feels as if there is no hope for relief, we can take courage from the example of this hope-filled woman of faith and be reassured by the Savior's words, "Daughter, be of good comfort: thy faith hath made thee whole; go in peace" (Luke 8:48).

Sorrow from Separation by Death

Dayna

When Roger died ten years ago, it felt like the sky was collapsing in on Dayna. But at least that time she had been given space to prepare. For months she held his hand pressing into hers, listening closely and trying hard to believe as he reminded her of how capable she was. He promised her that she was strong enough, that she could raise their seven adopted children without him. He plucked stars of hope for her, pinning back the black, falling sky with his love. As much as she hated the cancer that stole him from her, the slow progression of death had given her time to experience the most intense period of her mourning *with* him so when the funeral came, the grief didn't swallow her whole.

But this was entirely different. This time, death reared its ugly head like a cobra hidden in the grass, striking before there was even time to blink.

"You would have thought that my grief would have been worse with Roger. After all, I lost not only my husband, but our provider, my confidant and best friend. But the intensity of the pain when I learned Keioke had been killed in a car crash that night was unlike anything I have ever felt in my life. Sometimes I would go out into the fields at night and just yell. I was angry with God. I'm still so very angry."

Keioke was stubborn and fiery, as most of Dayna's teenagers had been. They had argued that night over a chore left half-done. When Keioke stormed from the house, Dayna moved to the front door and called out to her. She wanted Keioke to know she wasn't mad, that everything was fine between them. Whether Keioke heard her or not, Dayna never knew. She watched her drive away—her daughter never looking back.

Scriptural Accounts

Many women in the scriptures suffered grief from the death of loved ones: Mary and Martha lost their brother Lazarus, Ruth and Naomi suffered the untimely deaths of their husbands, and the widow of Nain mourned her only son, to name just a few. However, the most memorable death in scripture for all Christians is that of Jesus Christ. Each of the four gospels describe the terrible mourning Christ's loved ones endured, from His scattered Apostles, to His angelic mother at the foot of His cross, and the women anointing His body for burial. Mary Magdalene was found by the resurrected Lord weeping at His empty tomb, assuming that His detractors hated Him so much that they could not even leave His body to rest in peace.

Despite the Savior teaching His followers about His ultimate sacrifice through the Atonement and His impending suffering on the cross, His death was still horrific and shocking to His disciples. They had seen Him heal all manner of diseases, calm the elements, feed five thousand, and even raise people from the dead. The enormity of their grief over His death was deep and raw, their faith tested by the inability of their mortal experience to comprehend the ultimate and supreme power of the Son of God to lay down His life for us and pick it up again.

President Russell M. Nelson spoke about the sharp pangs created by the separation of death as he taught, "Death separates 'the spirit and the body [which] are the soul of man.' That separation evokes pangs of sorrow and shock among those left behind. The hurt is real.

Only its intensity varies. Some doors are heavier than others. The sense of tragedy may be related to age. Generally, the younger the victim, the greater the grief. Yet, even when the elderly or infirm have been afforded merciful relief, their loved ones are rarely ready to let go. The only length of life that seems to satisfy the longings of the human heart is life everlasting."[2]

All who enter into this life must eventually pass out of it. It is natural that we should grieve the departure. However, the miracle of the Savior's triumph over death should breathe hope into our hearts, filling us with comfort and conviction with the knowledge that these separations are temporary. Our sorrow from loss will be swallowed up in the joy of the resurrection of all mankind and the promise of eternity.

Suffering Due to the Agency of Another

Felicity and Daniel

"How is your daughter doing?" a coworker asked with deep concern in his eyes. Daniel assumed he was asking in general about Isabelle's launch into adulthood now that she was living on her own and attending the local university. "She's doing just fine." The standard answer came easily, although, truth be told, Isabelle had been far from fine for years. As the second daughter, she had always had to fight for her place, had always possessed a strong, feisty personality. But it had been over a decade since she had turned eight, and the flashes of fire in her eyes had gone from the occasional angry outburst to a near-constant smoldering of rage. For ages, Daniel and his wife, Felicity, had tried everything they could think of to get Isabelle to open up, but their daughter turned ice cold, locked her family out of her heart, and refused to let anyone in. The years passed, and their troubled little girl grew up, moved off to college, distant in both body and mind.

"Are you sure she's okay?" the co-worker pursued again with eyebrows raised. "Rape is such a traumatic event for the whole family."

Daniel felt as though he had been hit by a train. "Rape? What do you mean rape?"

In the coming hours and days, the shocking truths of years of abuse came out one by one like a jagged knife ripping a hole in the family's hearts, each new bit of information enlarging the increasingly painful wound. A trusted cousin. Molestation for years. Threats of violence from the perpetrator that kept their precious daughter in near-constant fear and shame daily for the past ten years. And now abuse from the hands of her first college boyfriend.

At last, clarity came to Felicity with the heavy price of the sickening knowledge. Isabelle's anger. Of course, the anger at everyone and everything. Understanding finally clicked into place after so many years of not knowing what had changed their child's emotions into a perpetual hurricane.

How could Felicity not have known? Why hadn't the Lord alerted her mother instincts? How could she ever forgive herself for not protecting her baby girl? It was too heavy to bear. And yet, the floodgates were now open. The truth, in all of its troubling facets, coupled with love and forgiveness, could begin to wash away the grime of a decade.

As Felicity and Daniel began to restore their relationship with their daughter, they realized boundaries needed to be drawn so she would not have to face her perpetrator unnecessarily. In an effort to support her healing, they confronted their extended family about the years of sexual abuse, but to their dismay, they found them completely in denial. "It takes two," Felicity's father insisted, implying that an innocent, eight-year-old girl was somehow responsible for the abuse at the hands of her fifteen-year-old cousin.

Felicity shared, "Probably the hardest part of the whole ordeal for my family has not been just the fall out and watching my daughter struggle. The hardest part was that my parents chose my sister and the perpetrator. When it all came out, we were told that if we wanted to be part of the family we had to say it didn't happen and go on with life like it was before. We were to ignore all my daughter's and, later, three other kids' pain and feelings—not to mention our own—and *pretend*. When we refused to accept that and chose to support our daughter, we became the subject of many lies [told by my parents] to anyone who would listen. That was the hardest part; their betrayal and being turned into the problem. All we ever asked them for was to try to understand and to not ask us to attend family functions that he would be part of, or to invite him to ours. That was it. As bad as his choices were, in many ways, my parents' choices have been as bad or worse for our family."

The effects of first one person's agency, and then an entire group's, introduced a pain into Felicity's household that has been multifaceted and long-lasting. In the end, Felicity and Daniel made the choice to protect their own family. They chose the relationships with their children over that of their parents. "It has not been an easy choice, but we have never regretted it for a moment."

Scriptural Accounts

Esther is one of only two women with their own book of scripture and is a perfect example of someone who is made to suffer due to the agency of others. After King Ahasuerus, a powerful Persian king, became angry with his queen and disposed of her, Esther was chosen to fill the empty space. However, the distinction of being a queen meant little in terms of freedom or stability. If she made even one wrong move, Esther could meet the same fate as her predecessor.

In a series of power plays made by the men of the court, the order was given for all the Jews in Persia to be slain. Little did King Ahasuerus know, his new bride was herself a Jew. Due to the greed and pride of others, Esther was placed in an extremely dangerous position. The decision was grim—save her people or save herself. Mordecai encouraged Esther with these memorable words, "Who knoweth whether thou art come to the kingdom for such a time as this?" (Esther 4:14). After earnest fasting and prayer, Esther put her trust, and her life, into the hands of God. Her notable virtue, faith, and courage carried her through and she was able to achieve safety for both herself and her people, the Jews.

We have all experienced instances when another person's choices have led to suffering in our lives. We can see this played out from the intimacy of our living rooms to the public stage of world politics. Rather than feeling helpless at our inability to control other people or organizations, we can take comfort in knowing that we are responsible for our own efforts. We have the agency to choose our actions and reactions in response to the circumstances of our lives—the power to make of it what we will. Like Queen Esther of old, we have the potential within us to have a tremendous impact for good.

* * *

You may have heard the expression "God won't give you more than you can handle," but based on the stories above, and perhaps established from our own experiences, that may feel untrue. Often, the burdens placed upon our shoulders are far heavier than we can carry alone. The Apostle Paul was a redeemed sinner who became a stalwart disciple of Christ, full of faith and conviction. Yet in Paul's second letter to the Corinthians he confessed, "For we would not, brethren, have you ignorant of our trouble . . . that we were pressed out of measure, above strength, insomuch that we despaired even of life" (2 Corinthians 1:8).

As Paul attests, our challenges often stretch us *above and beyond* our power to endure. But, be comforted. Our heartache is *never* beyond the might of our Heavenly Father. "But God is faithful: He will not suffer you to be tempted beyond that which ye are able to bear, but with the temptation will also make a way to escape, that ye may be able to bear it" (1 Corinthians 10:13). The word *temptation* in these verses can be substituted for the word *test*. Sometimes we hear the metaphor that life is a test. However, I prefer the thought that life is a classroom. Mistakes and trials don't affect our value and worth, but they can be learning spaces to teach us invaluable lessons of empathy and wisdom. Maybe we sign ourselves up for them, or perhaps they come through someone else's agency, but one thing is certain—we will not get through this life without them.

Heavenly Father never expected us to face these classes of adversity on our own. From the onset of His great plan of happiness, He prepared a Savior for us, expecting us to share the weight of our burdens with Him. "Come unto me, all ye that labour and are heavy laden," the Savior invited, "and I will give you rest. Take my yoke upon you, and learn of me; for I am meek and lowly in heart: and ye shall find rest unto your souls. For my yoke is easy, and my burden is light" (Matthew 11:28–30).

So, if suffering is a natural, universal part of life's classroom, why does it often feel as though we are the only one who has ever felt the way we do? Why do thoughts such as, "Why is this happening to me?" hit with such force in our moments of greatest shock and sorrow?

ENDNOTES

1. Robert D. Hales, "Your Sorrow Shall Be Turned to Joy," churchofjesuschrist.org/study/general-conference/1983/10/your-sorrow-shall-be-turned-to-joy?lang=eng, October 1983.
2. Russell M. Nelson, "Doors of Death, churchofjesuschrist.org/study/general-conference/1992/04/doors-of-death?lang=eng, April 1992.

CHAPTER 5

Why Me?

Phase 1: Victim

"If the very jaws of hell shall gape open the mouth wide after thee, know thou, my son, that all these things shall give thee experience, and shall be for thy good."

—Doctrine and Covenants 122:7

My husband and I recently took our children on a hike in southern Utah known as the Aspiration Trail. Situated among barren hills with prickly cacti and dull sagebrush, it seemed an unlikely spot to find other hikers. Yet, on the Saturday we arrived, we were surprised to see numerous groups picking their way slowly along, their heads bent low as they examined something on the trail. As it turns out, the hikers don't flock here to admire beautiful flora and fauna, but to enjoy the inspirational messages painted on rocks. The vast variety of notes range from an ocean scene encouraging, "Just keep swimming," to the popular saying, "It's a good day to have a good day," as well as an assortment of creative artwork of bizarre alien heads, beautiful sunrises, and glittery hearts.

Our little ones were delighted with each new stone, choosing a current favorite around each bend and hardly noticing the effort they were exerting in the excitement to get to the next motivating memo. As we approached another pair of painted rocks, the messages caused me to stop in my tracks. One rock read, "Why me?" And the other questioned, "Why not you?"

As I stared at those rocks, I wondered if the painter of the stones was a single person asking and answering their own question, or, if the original message had been only part one—a pleading, rhetorical *why me?* Perhaps the creator placed their query on the trail without hope of an answer. I played out an imaginary scene in my head, supposing another individual had come along, read the question, and cared enough to give the artist the profound answer—*why not you?* Though I had seen versions of this same debate in the past, it struck me anew that this age-old question, answered by way of another question, could change our entire perspective on the purpose of pain.

As we scramble for solid ground when our world is shaken, we often try to steady ourselves by finding answers. *Why me?* is a universal cry that highlights an urgent human craving for understanding. If we can just find a purpose, a *reason* behind our sorrows, it will somehow make them more tolerable. Meaninglessness feels unbearable. Thus, it is human nature that some of the first thoughts that cross our minds when faced with challenges formulate into some version of the question *why?* At its core, these pleas echo the same deep-seated longing for alternate options as first posed by Mother Eve's question, "Is there no other way?"

An interesting scenario from the book of Nephi makes me consider how the daughters of Ishmael may have felt about Eve's question and the purpose of their sufferings. To set the stage, Nephi's family is traveling through a barren wilderness not unlike, I imagine, the dusty setting of the Aspiration Trail. He and his brothers have been fighting amongst themselves, broken their hunting bows (which nearly leads to the starvation of the entire company), and mourned the death of Ishmael, the father of their wives. To say the journey has been rough would be a vast understatement. Nephi states, "And we did travel and wade through much affliction in the wilderness and our women did bear children in the wilderness" (1 Nephi 17:1).

This period of time must have been horrendous for the daughters of Ishmael. Imagine giving birth in a forsaken wasteland while weighed down by the family feud, hunger, and grief over the loss of a beloved parent. They must have felt so alone with their family patriarch dead and their new husbands in frequent conflict. I try to picture their reality as my own, leaving a home of prominence and comfort in the city of Jerusalem to follow my father obediently into the wilderness, be married to the only eligible males within hundreds of miles, only to find myself starving, pregnant, dirty, and exhausted. If I was one of the daughters of Ishmael, I think I would have been bitter. I think I would have questioned, "Was our father really inspired to come with Lehi's family? Was this actually God's plan for me? How could this possibly benefit any of us?"

It must have been supremely difficult for these newlyweds to trust their husbands who couldn't yet prove the wisdom in their expedition, especially those married to Laman and Lemuel, who did not even believe in their father's revelations or the wisdom of the exodus. I wonder if Nephi and his brothers felt like failures too. I wonder if they were embarrassed at the life they had roped these women into, unable at times to even provide for their temporal needs. As with Eve in the garden, I have so many questions for Ishmael's daughters.

It can be nigh impossible to keep a positive, faithful outlook when you're hit with one blow after another, especially if you're surrounded by hangry people who feel they have been dragged into a mess they didn't sign up for. At one time or another, nearly all the company complained. Yet, ever the optimist, Nephi documents, "And so great were the *blessings* of the Lord upon us that while we did live upon raw meat in the wilderness, our women did give plenty of suck for their children and were strong, yea, even like unto the men; and they began to bear their journeying without murmurings" (1 Nephi 17:2, emphasis added). It is astounding to me that after acknowledging the many afflictions they were facing, Nephi immediately follows up with how very blessed they had been. Nowhere does he convey a tone of "Why, Lord?" He simply accepts the adversity and makes the best of a hard deal, finding purpose in their hardships through his knowledge of God's eternal plan of happiness. His faith is bolstered as he looks for the good and reflects on their strengths rather than their weaknesses. And because of his example, the entire company is uplifted.

Just like Nephi and the daughters of Ishmael, we will all be presented with opportunities to choose how we will respond to pain when it inevitably comes knocking. But for most, we must first face and reconcile the *why me* questions in order to move forward in accepting the perspective of *why not you*? The initial disbelief and often overwhelming pain we feel at the onset of our trials was manifested in the heartbreaking stories shared by many of the women I interviewed.

Mikel

Mikel found herself asking the question "why?" countless times during her years of infertility. Coming from a large family of sisters and sisters-in-law starting families of their own with no challenges, Mikel found herself deeply embittered with each failed attempt to become pregnant and several unproductive fertility treatments. "It was so hard to see my sisters getting pregnant without even thinking about it. I worked in a pediatric office, and I would see these teenage moms coming in who, I felt, shouldn't be having kids, and I just felt so angry all the time. It got to the point that I couldn't even go to family functions. I couldn't hide my feelings, and it was just too much for me."

Mikel found herself questioning God's love for her. She wondered how He could possibly give babies to mothers who didn't want them while she desperately yearned to start her family. In her anger, she found herself drawn away from the Lord and being consumed with feelings of resentment. Why, of all her family, was this happening to her? Why, when she knew she could provide a loving home and be a devoted mother, was God denying her the opportunity to care for His children?

Nicole

Nicole felt as though she was on the verge of throwing up. She couldn't believe this was happening. The word *bankrupt* felt like a knockout after fighting tooth and nail against the looming opponent for so many years. How could this have happened when they had always tried to keep the commandments? They had always paid their tithing. They had always given without an expectation of reward.

For years her husband had served as bishop, attending to the poor and needy. He had readily given his signature for families in need of financial assistance while refusing to ask for any help of his own. They believed in being self-reliant. They believed in doing everything within their power to follow God's plan of providing for themselves. Painfully, they had watched other families who refused to work, waltz in with an air of complete ingratitude, and request welfare to pay for items that Nicole and her family had deprived themselves of for years in order to make ends meet. What was the line between being generous and helping all of God's children, while still expecting those in need to make an effort?

As Nicole and her husband sat at the table, the stark numbers in front of them appeared cold and uncaring. They could no longer avoid the reality that no matter how hard they worked, there was no other way out of this pit. She covered her face with her hands, despair seeping through the cracks in her fingertips. Why couldn't the Lord have prevented this from happening? How would they ever recover? The injustice felt wildly unfair.

Julia

For Julia, the question of "why?" came as she spent years struggling with singleness. There was nothing that she wanted more desperately than to be a loving wife and mother. She tried her best to make her life as fulfilling as possible with work, pursuing higher education goals, and fostering meaningful relationships. At the time, women were encouraged to wait until marriage before receiving their temple endowment, barring Julia from making further covenants and excluding her from the blessing of seeking refuge in temple service.

As her youthful years ticked by, she began to despair, wondering why her righteous desires to follow God's plan for marriage and family were being denied her. "I often felt sorrow during those years, because I worried that no one seemed to want me." Depression was a frequent companion as Julia finally admitted to herself that the family she hungered for so fiercely might never be realized in her lifetime. The possibility that her dreams were just that—an unobtainable illusion—threatened to snuff out the tiny flame of hope she had protected and nurtured for so long.

LaRae

LaRae was the middle child wedged between three older and three younger siblings. Her brother Kenny, one of her best friends, was just eighteen months older than her. As LaRae prepared to enter high school, she already felt she had a leg up socially being "Kenny's sister," as everyone knew and loved the vivacious, athletic, kind Kenny. That summer Kenny was in top physical condition as he passed a grueling lifeguard training and prepared for high school sports with high hopes. However, two weeks before school started, he began to be uncharacteristically sluggish. Bruises appeared on his body. He complained of bloody noses and backaches. A local doctor said not to worry. It was probably just a virus.

LaRae remembers waking early in the morning a week before school started. She wanted to go back to bed, as her precious days of sleeping in were drawing to a close, but something compelled her to get up. As she sat in the kitchen preparing a bowl of cereal, her father rushed in the back door, his face pale and harried.

"Daddy, what is it?" LaRae asked.

"It's Kenny. I just carried him to the car. He hemorrhaged in the night and he's lost so much blood. Take care of your siblings. We have to get to the hospital immediately."

Despite being the middle child, responsibility weighed heavily on LaRae as questions and gut-churning worry for her beloved brother raced through her mind. Within hours Kenny was diagnosed with leukemia and transferred to an ambulance that sped from Southern Utah to Salt Lake City to receive help. Before the ambulance had even gone a hundred miles, Kenny passed away.

Sitting in her living room more than fifty years after the tragedy, LaRae shook her head with eyes full of tears. "It was just so shocking. Why Kenny? He was the best of us. Everyone knew it. Why would God take such a bright light? I just couldn't wrap my head around it. Sometimes, I still can't."

Michelle

As the shock of the judge's decision began to wear off, Michelle felt the rage boiling within her. She felt like she could tear a building apart, brick by brick, with her bare hands. How could they possibly send these helpless foster children back into that despicable home, seeing what they had seen, knowing what they knew? Where was the justice? Where was God in this?

The social worker caught up with her in the parking lot, and all of the anguish flew out of Michelle's mouth in a torrent of sobs and screams. "How can they do this to them? How?!" The woman shook her head and said matter-of-factly, "Don't worry, these kids will be back soon. It's only a matter of time before they'll be taken again."

Michelle didn't realize her heart could sink lower. There was the confirmation she had known and yet feared. These precious children would be abused and neglected again. The same as before. Probably worse. She tried not to imagine Brooklyn—*her* Brooklyn—back in that hellish environment. She sobbed and pleaded with the social worker, "What can we possibly do?"

* * *

For Mikel, Nicole, Julia, LaRae, Michelle, and virtually every woman I interviewed, there were always the *why me* questions. When we find ourselves asking any version of *why*, it is an indication that we are somewhere at the beginning of our Growth Through Grief journey. The ultimate goal of this continuum is determining how to find value in the sorrows of our lives. In order to grow from our adversity, we must learn to navigate through three basic phases: Victim, Survivor, and Contributor, choosing to develop into a stronger individual despite, or perhaps *because*, of our grief. As we reflect on our lives, virtually all of us can identify a trial we have or are currently striving to overcome. To diagnose where our mindset currently dwells regarding our challenges and to set goals for further healing, we must first understand the natural progression of these three phases of Growth Through Grief.

The first and most common phase of sorrow is that of Victim. In this frame of mind, we explore the *why me* questions. Here, we wrestle with our natural inclinations to mourn versus a desire to immediately push away a trial. We also sort out helpful versus unhelpful sorrow (clean pain versus dirty pain), topics we will delve into further in the coming chapters. Unfortunately, the word *victim* has quite a negative connotation. We hear spiteful phrases such as, "She's just playing the victim," which evokes pessimistic feelings, making victimhood a negative narrative. However, the way I would define a victim is "a person who is suffering from any circumstance that (they perceive) has negatively affected their life."

For many, Victim Mindset is a result of a violation of trust. When trust is betrayed in major ways, by Mother Nature, God, and especially by family (through abuse, divorce, or neglect) our cognitive development is impacted in profound ways, particularly in childhood before age eight. Literally, our brains are rewired to be on the defense.

My father, Dr. David Bush, has been a psychologist for more than forty years. As we discussed the Growth Through Grief mindset, he explained further:

> As a result of broken trust, those abused, hurt, or confused in those early childhood years are prone to Victim status. Of course, you can find many exceptions, but you can find more data linking both childhood and adult dysfunction to these traumatic events. Post-traumatic growth (in place of post-traumatic stress disorder) requires not just a shift in mental attitude, but often significant work to re-frame the experience. Adults have the mental capacity to analyze their pain and move on, but children do not and often establish patterns that set them up for further abuse in adulthood. Or they create self-defeating patterns of behavior or ineffective coping strategies such as substance abuse, manipulation and lying, defensiveness and relationship challenges. Sometimes, we just want people to 'go to work' to fix things and right the wrong, but trust precedes work. It is hard to accept responsibility for the things you might be able to change until you have faith that any effort or action on your part will make a difference. When children are subject to situations out of their control (especially children in foster care, removed from abuse and then too often returned to abuse) they engage in all manner of self-sabotage. Hence, the *only* source of faith or trust, is trusting in a power greater than yourself if you hope to heal and learn from suffering and move from Victim status to Survivor or Contributor.[1]

For some, the Victim phase may be a lifelong pursuit as they seek to overcome trauma that has literally altered their brain. Professional help may be required in order to progress. One of my interviewees was unable to talk about the agonizing miscarriage of her child without having a complete emotional meltdown until she met with a psychologist. With his professional expertise, she underwent EMDR, a form of treatment that helped her process the post-traumatic stress associated with her loss. Until seeking treatment, she felt stuck in victimhood, but since receiving assistance, she has now gained the ability to deal with those traumatic memories in a healthy manner.

For others, no treatment or counseling may be necessary, as their Victim phase will be short lived. Their personality may be such that they are capable of moving through this phase relatively quickly. They may be able to put their *why me* thoughts to rest by answering their questions with faith-promoting or positive thoughts. The Victim Phase can also cut short when an individual chooses to allow themselves to feel their natural emotions instead of resisting or hiding from their pain.

JoAnne

JoAnne has developed the skill to sift through the strong feelings attached to her challenges and use a more logical approach to resolving them. "I've learned to keep a handle on my emotions. When I am faced with a problem, I almost always have the ability to analyze it quickly, recognize what needs to be done to fix it, and then I take the next step forward. I don't spend a lot of time wallowing."

Perhaps JoAnne may not have felt the need to cultivate this capacity, if not for her introduction to deep and lasting grief at the tender age of eleven when her beloved father passed away. After his death, she found her grief so intense that she could hardly talk about him with others for many years. "I experienced confusion, fear, deep sadness, loneliness, and longing for him. However, I will say that I never felt anger at God because my father was dead. I was able to put my trust in God's plan and rely on my faith in Jesus Christ. The hope that they offer to all of us has helped me learn to grieve without becoming incapacitated or bound down by emotions that come with grief."

Although it has been fifty-four years since his passing, JoAnne believes that a spiritual gift was born from the sorrow of losing him. She explained, "I do believe that part of the blessing I have been given, to be able to look not just emotionally but also practically at hardships and then see a way forward, is truly a spiritual gift. I have had many other experiences that have caused great sorrow and pain, but not to the point of being overwhelmed. Always I feel relief through prayer. God has been very good to me."

* * *

For many people, especially women, this systematic approach to moving through the initial Victim Phase is not as readily attainable, nor does it suit their natural proclivity to let their emotions spend more time on center stage. Sometimes we *want* and *need* to stay in a casualty space while our minds and hearts are reeling, trying our best to make sense of what has happened and create a new plan for moving forward. We might not be ready to be strong or to jump right into the healing process. We may simply need time—and that's okay! Neither a swift nor a slow approach is better than the other for moving through Phase One of Victimhood. Just as no two people are the same, neither are two experiences with grief or learning to cope with it.

In the last general conference address before his death, Elder Joseph B. Wirthlin said, "You may feel singled out when adversity enters your life. You shake your head and wonder, 'Why me?' But the dial on the wheel of sorrow eventually points to each of us. At one time or another, everyone must experience sorrow. No one is exempt."[2] Although I never found myself asking, "Why me?" per se, my variations were, "Why didn't we take the babies sooner? Should we have made a different choice? Why was one son saved and not the other?"

* * *

New Year's Day dawned on January 1, 2016, crisp and bright. The sun seemed to transmit a near-tangible energy of fresh possibilities as it filtered through the intricate patterns of frost on our windows. I awoke flooded with excitement. I could feel in my core that something life changing was coming. "This is going to be a *big* year!" I enthusiastically told my husband.

Little did I know, *big* was hardly the word for it. *Humongous* was more like it, as just months later I was waddling around with a massive forty-pound beach ball on my stomach, enormously pregnant with identical twin boys.

The moment I suspected I was pregnant, something deep within me whispered I was carrying twins. I felt no surprise, just a wild mixture of

trepidation and excitement when our first ultrasound showed two perfectly round heads on the screen. With our young daughters doing a
happy dance in the corner of the room, Burke and I laughed the slightly
hysterical cackle of the convicted. We knew we were plunging head-long
into the furnace with soon-to-be four kids under the age of five. The
news spread like wildfire through our families and friends, their elation
and delight emblazing us with courage for the undoubtedly rough, yet
rewarding inferno ahead. We embraced the reality of a double blessing of
both increased joy and chaos. But whatever intuition had ensured me it
would be a "big" year and informed me I was growing twins well before
any medical data confirmed it, that same motherly instinct also alerted
me that something was wrong.

The feeling would not abate, and the near-constant fatigue, illness,
and worry for our babies left me completely drained. Searching for
relief, I asked Burke and my father to give me a priesthood blessing
of comfort. Speaking on behalf of our Heavenly Father, Burke laid
his gentle hands on my head and blessed me that I would feel peace,
that I would know that we were being watched over by family on both
sides of the veil. I breathed a sigh of relief, assuming the blessing was
complete. To my dismay, Burke continued on with words that sent my
heart racing with anxiety.

"Emily, this pregnancy will continue to be a bumpy road full of
mental turmoil and anguish. There will be many difficult decisions to
be made." Here he paused, as though waiting for inspiration to come,
sorting out his personal feelings from the message the Lord wanted
him to convey. "But, Emily, in the end, these babies will come whole
and healthy."

The blessing went on, but all I can remember is repeating in my
mind the phrase "whole and healthy." I swallowed back the tears. I
could handle a bumpy road. I could handle mental turmoil and
anguish as long as the babies came whole and healthy.

By our twenty-week ultrasound, the bumpy road had hit in full
force. As the OB noted a major, forty-percent growth discrepancy
between our Twin A (Aiden) and Twin B (Alan), it felt as though we
were standing at the base of a mountain of grief, a precarious rockslide
above, rumbling dangerously with each new tremor of bad news. We
were sent to a high-risk pregnancy specialist, and after extensive monitoring, we were informed that our babies were connected through a

series of blood vessels that had grown together in their mutual placenta. This linkage had caused twin-twin transfusion syndrome (TTTS), a sharing of blood between the twins that created a donor and recipient relationship. While one baby lost precious nutrients, the other's heart could overwork from the excess blood filling his body, putting both at risk for demise. If one baby passed, the other would continue to pump blood and nutrients into the dead fetus, resulting in high risks of severe brain damage or death for the surviving twin.

The stones of adversity began to unsettle one by one. Each cold diagnosis began as mere pebbles, sharp and stinging as they made contact, yet gaining momentum and size until whole threatening boulders cascaded down. Over the next several weeks of heaviness, we dodged to avoid the worst blows, trying everything we possibly could to help our struggling sons.

At twenty-five weeks, with our options running out, we were sent to Los Angeles, California, for an emergency surgery with Dr. Ramen Chmait, one of only five doctors in the United States at the time who could perform revolutionary intrauterine procedures. After a lengthy assessment, Dr. Chmait informed us that our situation was grave. Not only did the boys have TTTS, but another factor was also complicating their growth. While Alan's umbilical cord had attached perfectly to their shared placenta, Aiden's was "unfavorable," essentially dangling off the bottom of the placenta and receiving only the dregs to sustain him.

We were given four options: abort the pregnancy completely, tie off the umbilical cord to Baby A to leave Baby B with all the nutrients, undergo dangerous intrauterine surgery to sever the connected blood vessels, or return home and try to take the babies via emergency C-section before one or both of the twins passed from the effects of TTTS.

I will never forget the way I felt as we sat in that office. The crushing weight of the rocky mountain came barreling into us. We felt swallowed whole by a raging avalanche of despair.

It was six o'clock in the evening. The worn-out staff was ready to close the office for the night, and we had to decide immediately if we would schedule surgery at five o'clock the next morning.

The sympathetic staff showed us to a conference room where Burke and I could discuss in private. As the door closed, we collapsed into one another, the magnitude of the decision boring down upon us. With no other hope but our hope in Christ, we kneeled and poured out our hearts, pleading for knowledge as to how we should proceed. The comfort and direction we sought came to us almost immediately in the remembrance of the priesthood blessing I had received months earlier. "Whole and healthy," we were reminded. "The babies will come whole and healthy." With renewed faith, I clung to the promise of those words and prepared for surgery.

Using a microscopic laser, Dr. Chmait utilized his carefully honed surgical skills to enter the uterus and sever the twins' inter-connected blood veins. It was risky and dangerous, but thanks to the remarkable doctor and his staff, the miraculous surgery was a success. Though he could not change the poor positioning of Aiden's umbilical cord, the procedure stopped the donor and recipient relationship, allowing each baby a separate fate, no longer tied to the survival or demise of the other.

The surgery had granted us a momentary triumph, a temporary pause in the rockslide. Before making the journey home, Dr. Chmait urged us to try our hardest not to intervene too soon or take the babies too early. If we could wait until at least thirty-two weeks gestation, the risk for spina bifida, blindness, cerebral palsy, and a host of other ailments would be drastically reduced. He reminded us that while Baby A was still fighting for his life, Baby B was essentially an innocent bystander and growing perfectly. Choosing to take the babies early would inflict upon him lifelong health problems that he otherwise might never encounter if given time to develop normally.

How could we choose to let one twin suffer over the other, to value the life of Twin A or Twin B more than his brother? "Whole and healthy, Emily," I reminded myself again.

Over the next six weeks, we maintained bi-weekly ultrasounds, stress tests, steroid shots, and partial bed rest. However, Baby A's levels continued to be poor and his growth severely restricted. Each week our perinatologist would remind us, "Baby A is not doing well. He most likely won't be here at our next appointment." Each week we carried the heaviness of that heartache but worked hard to maintain our faith that God had a plan for us and our babies and that all would turn out well in the end.

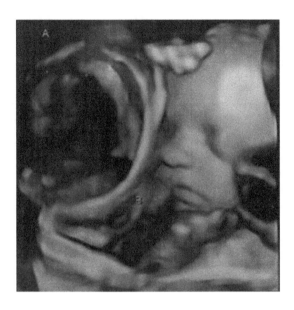

At thirty-one weeks, our perinatologist took a remarkable 3D image of our sons. We were all elated to see Twin A, his heart still beating, his fire still burning, cupping his brother's sweet face in his hands, their heads lovingly pressed together. Against all odds, we had made it! With an overwhelming sense of gratitude, triumph, and relief, we scheduled our C-section, overjoyed that we would soon be meeting our sons. Our bumpy road appeared to be at an end at last.

ENDNOTES

1. David Bush, personal email to Emily Adams, May 1, 2020.
2. Joseph B. Wirthlin, "Come What May, and Love It," churchofjesus-christ.org/study/general-conference/2008/10/come-what-may-and-love-it?lang=eng, October 2008.

CHAPTER 6

Perfected in Him

"Yea, come unto Christ,
and be perfected in him."

—Moroni 10:32

The chilly waters off the coast of the Pacific Northwest captivated international attention in August of 2018 as an orca whale, nicknamed Tahlequah, was documented driving the lifeless body of her newborn calf to the water's surface again, and again, in a fruitless attempt to breathe life into the still form. After up to eighteen months of gestation, whale calves are often supported by the mother and other female whales from the pod, assisting them above the waves and encouraging the baby to take their first breath of air. In what became termed as a "tour of grief" the world watched the heartbreaking story unfold as Tahlequah clung stubbornly to hope, refusing to eat or rest as she nosed her baby relentlessly to the surface for a record-setting seventeen-day, 1,000-mile sojourn through the sea, the longest display of marine mourning ever observed.[1]

The bond between a mother and its baby is one of the most innate, organic relationships in all of nature. This exhibition of grief, demonstrated by a behaviorally complex and intelligent species, evoked intense feelings of empathy the world over. Logically, individuals were

See Me. Watercolor painting by Lori Christopher.
Used with permission from the artist.

touched as they observed a mother going through an intense lamentation process for her offspring as these emotions could easily be seen mirrored in our own species, as could the behavior of the pod. Rather than leaving behind their suffering sister to carry this burden alone, many of the other females of Tahlequah's pod began taking turns holding the deceased baby aloft, allowing the exhausted mama time to eat, rest, and recover before she would inevitably return to pick up her cross once more.

As I curiously watched news feeds for updates on the story to unfold each day that August, my heart was especially tender as we approached Aiden's second angelversary. I thought of the many women who had swum tight around me during the agonizing days, weeks, and months following Aiden's loss, buoying me up, forcing me to breathe.

After nearly three weeks, Tahlequah finally succumbed to the reality of her loss, and the beloved body of her baby slipped below the waves for the last time. When I read the headline, I mourned afresh that day, knowing all too well the feeling of utter defeat and despair that bears down on a mother when that final, inevitable goodbye comes in a tidal wave of sorrow. As President Nelson so astutely observed, "The only way to take sorrow out of death is to take love out of life."[2] No matter our species, we mourn because we love.

In a case such as Tahlequah's, we can watch the scene play out in nature and clinically understand her reaction as instinctive. Likewise, we may observe another person's loss and compassionately accept their resulting grief as innate and normal. But have you noticed that when it comes to our own grieving, the perspective becomes skewed? Instead of permitting ourselves the same compassion we would to a friend (or even a stranger) undergoing a trial, we instead chastise ourselves for feeling emotions that are perfectly within the realm of inherent, biological responses. We may be capable of acknowledging legitimate pain in others, while ineffective at granting that precious gift of grace to ourselves.

This inability to be lenient with our expectations for ourselves may be an indication of an internal struggle with toxic perfectionism. Essentially, if we fall into perfectionism, we become hungry for approval and believe that our value is conditional, based on how well we perform. This causes a proclivity to evaluate our worth in comparison with others. *Psychology Today* states, "For perfectionists, life is an endless report card on accomplishments or looks. A one-way ticket to unhappiness, perfectionism is typically accompanied by depression. What makes perfectionism so toxic is that while those in its grip desire success, they are most focused on avoiding failure."[3]

To clarify, perfectionism is *not* the same as doing your best. It is not setting goals and reaching for improvement. Instead, it becomes a (often subconscious) means by which we deprive ourselves of feelings of satisfaction and fulfillment when we have performed well. Rather than having a realistic perception of what is fine and complete, we fixate on what is missing or wrong. This slanted mindset impacts every area in our lives: work, hobbies, relationships, education, worship, mental health, and our happiness.

Members of The Church of Jesus Christ of Latter-Day Saints are not immune to this social illness. In fact, in prevalent ways we are more prone to the trap of toxic perfectionism than other groups based solely upon our core theology that we, as the children of a Heavenly Father, are striving to become like Him—to become godlike—to become perfect. Members of the Church who seem to struggle keenly with feelings of worth often have taken literally the scripture "Be ye therefore perfect" (Matthew 5:48).

Rather than viewing perfection as an eternal goal, perfectionists berate themselves unjustly when they fall short, believing they should be flawless *now*. The widespread misunderstanding of this scripture and the cultural spread of perfectionism led Elder Jeffrey R. Holland to remind us that the scripture could have read, "Be ye therefore perfect . . . eventually."[4]

The problem with a perfectionist mindset, particularly regarding suffering, is that it twists our ability to grieve properly. The challenges we face may vary in their levels of severity, duration, and complexity, but each will undoubtedly create thoughts along the lines of, "My life plans have now been changed in an unexpected, negative way." This thought is most often accompanied by a sense of loss. A consciousness of loss could arise from something as trivial as feeling disappointment when plans are canceled with a friend, to the sting of being passed over for a job promotion, or as earth-shattering as the suicide of a loved one. Regardless of the circumstance, there is power when we stop resisting our emotions and accept disappointment as a natural, human reaction to trials.

When things go wrong in our lives, we often compound the pain of the experience by trying to respond in a way that will allow us to keep up the perfectionist façade. For example, as members of the Church, this may play out when our inborn feelings of sorrow battle with our desire to react in a way that is in harmony with gospel teachings. It is good and right to try to emulate virtues such as patience, perseverance, and faith during times of trial. However, forcing ourselves, or others, to jump immediately to those ideal qualities can often be damaging to our healing. This is especially true if the effort is born out of a sense of obligation to keep up appearances or to meet unrealistic expectations about how we "should" react in the moment of distress.

I remember sitting in church one Sunday feeling weighed down with sadness that yet another month had passed and I still wasn't pregnant. I had always hoped to have my children about two years apart, but it had been well over a year of trying, and I stressed that perhaps our oldest daughter may be our one and only. As I quietly lamented internally, the quintessential "attitude of gratitude" hymn, "Count Your Blessings," was loudly pealed out by the enthusiastic organist. I looked around at all the happy faces smiling as they sang, "Count your blessings name them one by one, and it will surprise you what the Lord hath done."[5] Now, instead of just feeling melancholy over our temporary infertility, I felt a coat of guilt settle over me like a dirty blanket. How dare I feel sad when scores of women had not had the opportunity to have any children at all? There was my bright-eyed three-year-old, swinging her legs joyfully to the upbeat song; happy, healthy, and smart as a whip. Wasn't I grateful for her? Didn't I realize how richly blessed we had been? If I was more faithful, surely, I could trust in God's timing and stop my mental whimpering.

Right then, my still-aching heart needed to feel sorrow for the disappointment of unmet plans. Yet my deeply instilled upbringing of faith doggedly told me that an attitude adjustment was all I needed to overcome my problem. Instead of recognizing that my longing for more children was grounds to feel legitimate sadness, my perfectionist tendencies of wanting to be the best possible follower of Christ harped in my mind, declaring that I was selfish and faithless. While *eventually* I would be able to use a sunny outlook to help with this particular worry, in that moment, I couldn't paste on a smile and pretend that I was in a state of mind to be grateful for this circumstance. *Eventually,* I would be able to count my blessings, to see the Lord's hand in my life. But today, I just needed to hurt.

When the innate *why me* questions arise, many of us don't allow ourselves time and space to consciously investigate those queries without feeling guilt. We may think that the questions in themselves equal weakness or doubt—that thereby *we* are frail and faithless. So, to avoid any semblance of uncertainty, we may choose to take our inquiries, along with any unpleasant feelings of shock, grief, or anger, and unconsciously shove them aside with thoughts such as, "If I allow myself to question, it must mean I am not fully converted." Or, "If I feel sad about this loss, I must not have a full testimony of gospel principle X, Y, or Z."

This incongruence between our natural inclination to feel loss and our Latter-day Saint bred, faith-in-all-circumstances tenacity can lead to a serious tug-of-war of heart versus head. Our heart demands that we *feel*, that we experience this sorrow in the way that our body and soul need to. However, our head, or rather our social and cultural experiences, can often dam up these emotions, refusing to let them be felt. This battle of head and heart is termed "resistance" and can be incredibly damaging to our mental, emotional, and physical health.

Clearly, our doctrine does not promote this repression. A true understanding of Christ's grace teaches that His power can work within us *during* our struggle. His Atonement is the balm in the midst of our pain, rather than a bandage applied as an afterthought following it.

One of my favorite stories of Christ is when He receives news that His dear friend Lazarus is critically ill. Rather than rushing to heal him, Christ intentionally delays His journey to Bethany, knowing that this trial has happened to reveal the glory of God (see John 11:4). Days later, when He finally arrives, Martha, sister of Lazarus and a disciple of Christ, comes out to meet Him. She is overcome with the sorrow of their loss and possibly feeling reproachful of the Savior when she censures, "Lord, if thou hadst been here, my brother had not died" (John 11:21). Later, her sister Mary repeats the same accusation, falling down and weeping at the feet of Jesus.

Despite Christ's internal knowledge that He is minutes away from performing one of His greatest miracles, that Lazarus will be raised from the dead, He still gives Himself space to grieve and show proper sympathy for the pain of these beloved women: "When Jesus therefore saw her weeping, and the Jews also weeping which came with her, he groaned in the spirit, and was troubled . . . Jesus wept" (John 11:33, 35).

We would do well to remember this scene. The Son of God, the only perfect person who has ever walked this Earth, took time to mourn. Christ wept, and so can we.

Shame comes as a result of resisting those natural emotions. It spreads its sickening tendrils through our minds, whispering one of Satan's most powerful lies, that we *shouldn't* allow ourselves that space for grieving. That we should hide our scars and our tears. We can, and often do, buy into the lie of perfectionism that says only broken people hurt. We may think that if we were a stronger person, then we could overcome this challenge or these emotions simply by our willpower. If only we pray harder, study our scriptures better, or minister more fully, then somehow we will be immune to grief.

Yet, I have learned from painful experience that resistance and shame are the least effective road we can take toward healing. Pushing away our uncomfortable emotions will only lead to further pain. Repression is often not even a conscious choice and can manifest itself in our actions such as overeating, spending more time at the office, shopping, or even just "being busy" in order to avoid distressing feelings or troubling situations. Though we may think we have successfully side-stepped the inconvenience and "weakness" of feeling sorrow at the time, I can promise you that no matter how long it takes—days or months or years—those caged emotions will never leave you in peace if they are not addressed. And though patient, grief will not be silenced forever.

Jamie Anderson is attributed with saying, "Grief, I've learned, is really just love. It's all the love you want to give, but cannot. All of that unspent love gathers up in the corners of your eyes, the lump in your throat, and in that hollow part of your chest. Grief is just love with no place to go."[6] Unfortunately, if we don't recognize that it is actually *love* that is trying to break through, we can bury those most precious and tender feelings in a blind attempt to smother the pain that, in reality, walks hand-in-hand with love.

The priesthood blessing I had received on behalf of our twins did not result in two whole and healthy babies in this life. As I confronted the initial shock of that reality, I found myself facing a very difficult decision. Either I believed in priesthood blessings, or I did not. Either I had faith that this particular blessing was founded on eternal principles and remained true, or it was all an illusion. I had to decide for myself if the blessing I had clung to as my lifeline during the hell of those long, arduous months was real. That my sons were indeed both "whole and healthy" with one residing on an opposite side of the veil than the other.

With this decision lay a testimony teetering on the brink of extinction or launching into the stratosphere of uncharted possibilities for personal growth.

In that critical moment, I chose to believe what the Spirit whispered to me. I chose faith. Faith that our son was whole. Faith that Aiden's mission was different from Alan's. Faith that I would see him again. Faith that there was purpose in the agony of losing him.

But without making a conscious decision, I also chose resistance and repression. I would believe, but I would not allow the *what if's* to enter in. I would not entertain the *why me's*. I had two small daughters and a premature twinless twin who needed me. I did not have the luxury of falling into emotional dysfunction to heal properly, or so my toxic perfectionism insisted. I would not allow this raging hole of grief in my heart to consume me. I bowed my back and dug my heels deep into my soul, determination to be what I professed to believe coursing through me. I caged my primitive emotions and threw away the key.

For many of the women I interviewed, this was an all too familiar experience.

Faith

When I interviewed Faith, I assumed we would discuss the grief and fear she had confronted when she underwent a dangerous operation. However, Faith completely changed my preconceived notions and verified that while a person, or a marriage, may look perfect on the surface, we are often unaware of the unseen burdens they may carry.

For Faith, the greatest sorrow of her life turned out not to be her health challenges. Instead, a greater burden arose when her world was turned upside down upon the discovery of her husband's pornography addiction. Despite Scott's sincere yearning to overcome the vice-like enslavement of addiction, the constant gnawing of distrust began to erode Faith's feelings of self-worth and their marital peace. This was not the ideal temple marriage she had envisioned.

However, Faith refused to let herself grieve over her crushed vision of a smooth eternal companionship. Though surgery had healed her physical maladies, Faith slowly found herself growing cold; the damage of Scott's addiction threatening to freeze her love completely in order to protect herself from further anguish. "For a long time, I saw expressing and feeling emotions as dramatic and a weakness. Because I had the gospel, I thought I should feel happiness all the time. I thought that I shouldn't feel sad, or rather, I wouldn't *allow* myself to feel sad. I became numb so I could pretend that everything was okay."

Whether consciously or not, Faith was caught in the web of perfectionism, both privately and socially. The shame she and her husband felt for his addiction resulted in a detrimental repression. With Scott's issue a secret, both he and Faith could not receive the support and treatment that they needed to heal. Rather than risk the acknowledgment that they needed help, the couple soldiered on, limping through the battlefield of his addiction, waiting for the next land mine to explode.

Brie

Growing up, Brie thought most moms stayed in bed all day. Chronic back pain had led her mother to become addicted to opioids and, later, alcohol. Her mother continued to abuse heavy meds during an unexpected pregnancy and was advised by the doctors to abort the baby as, almost certainly, there would be consequences. Miraculously, caboose baby Brie became child number ten in her family; beautiful, intelligent, and fully functioning. However, her home was anything but functional.

"My dad was completely in denial that my mom had a serious problem. In so many ways, he enabled her addictions by bringing her home from recovery programs too soon and making excuses for her. He was a workaholic. I really think, mostly, so he could escape from home and pretend like everything was okay."

Brie's dad was fully caught up in the perfectionist image. For many years, he blamed his wife's problems on her health, rather than her addictions. He fooled others, and perhaps even himself, that they were an ideal LDS family. "Sure, we went to church," Brie said with a shake of the head, "but we didn't really live it. We didn't read scriptures or pray as a family. My dad was a rule follower, so he had us go to all our meetings, but it didn't seem to really sink in."

Brie felt like she was living a double life of sorts. Their family presented a put-together front: happy smiles outside, heartache within. Not only was Brie's mother neglectful as a result of her addictions, but as time went on, she became increasingly abusive both physically and emotionally. As a teenager, Brie's self-esteem began to suffer, especially when her mother would say hurtful things about her birth being an accident.

Deep emotional wounds were formed in Brie's psyche from the poor choices of her parents that have haunted her into adulthood. "Because of my dysfunctional home, I didn't want to get married. But then I met Skyler. He knew all about being raised in a home with an alcoholic mother, which is why he ended up in foster care. Thankfully, he was rescued by truly good people. He was introduced to the gospel, and it completely changed his life. He served a mission, and we were married in the temple. He has been such an amazing example to me that we can overcome hard things and we can choose to have a beautiful life."

Brie had siblings who, due to their troubling upbringing, went on to have challenges of their own, often struggling with the same addictions that they loathed in their mother. "I have siblings who have chosen another path." Brie shared, "One of my sisters recently lost custody of her kids, and when we visited, she blamed all of her current problems on experiences we had with our mom. And I just don't believe that. Skyler and I have decided our pasts are an explanation, but they are not an excuse."

Brie has decided that her testimony will be *real*. Her children will know that they were wanted and are loved fiercely. The happiness in her marriage and home will be genuine, rather than smoke and mirrors to maintain an illusion of perfection.

Cassie

One phrase I frequently heard throughout the interviewing process was, "I've never shared this with anyone before." Cleansing tears often followed as pent-up stories of anguish spilled out of trembling lips that had held these damaging secrets for so long. Sometimes, for decades.

Several weeks after I had interviewed Cassie, she approached me at a church function and pulled me aside for a private word. "I just want you to know that our conversation stirred something up in me that I didn't have any idea was still bothering me. When I got home, my husband asked if I had told you about our daughter's car accident and I said, 'No, I forgot.' He asked if I had told you about another recent trial, and I said, 'Well, no, I didn't even think about it.' It made me realize that the emotional and mental abuse I experienced as a child and teenager, that I thought were ancient history, were still lingering with me after all these many, many years. I mean, I'm in my seventies now, for heaven's sake! I had no idea how much they still weighed on me until you gave me the chance to talk about any sorrow I wanted to. It just goes to show you never know the things you are still holding onto!"

* * *

When we try the perfectionist route, either denying that our pain is real so we can maintain the illusion of wholeness, or, seeking to solve our problems entirely on our own by pounding the weakness out of ourselves, we will be disappointed. The truth is, there has only ever been one perfect person, and it is He who stands with arms out-stretched, perfectly imperfect nail prints on the palms of His hands, beckoning for us to fall into His embrace, safe and whole once more.

In *Shadowlands*, a play about the life of C.S. Lewis, William Nicholson wrote:

> Self-sufficiency is the enemy of salvation. If you are self-sufficient, you have no need of God. If you have no need of God, you do not seek Him. If you do not seek Him, you will not find Him. God loves us, so He makes us the gift of suffering. Through suffering, we release our hold on the toys of this world and know our true good lies in another world. We're like blocks of stone, out of which the sculptor carves the forms of men. The blows of His chisel, which hurt us so much, are what makes us perfect. The suffering in the world is not the failure of God's love for us; it is that love in action.[7]

If we try to conquer our sorrows, trials, and imperfections on our own, we will undoubtedly fail. Every time. But, if we rely on the arm of He who is mighty to save, we can, in time, become perfect with Him. The prophet Moroni admonished, "Yea, come unto Christ, and be perfected in him" (Moroni 10:32).

For Faith, Brie, Cassie, myself, and so many of us, the powerful undercurrent of unacknowledged grief can run deeply through our souls, affecting us in ways we would be shocked to recognize. At some point, this subconscious interference becomes a necessity to address, but when, where, and how we go about facing our grief is an intensely personal experience.

ENDNOTES

1. Lori Cuthbert and Douglas Main, "Orca Mother Drops Calf, After Unprecedented 17 Days of Mourning," *National Geographic.com*, nationalgeographic.com/animals/2018/08/orca-mourning-calf-killer-whale-northwest-news/.

2. Russell M. Nelson, "Doors of Death, churchofjesuschrist.org/study/general-conference/1992/04/doors-of-death?lang=eng, April 1992.

3. "Psych Basics: Perfectionism," *Psychology Today*, 1 Mar. 2013, psychologytoday.com/basics/perfectionism.

4. Jeffrey R. Holland, "Be Ye Therefore Perfect—Eventually," churchofjesuschrist.org/study/general-conference/2017/10/be-ye-therefore-perfect-eventually?lang=eng, October 2017.

5. Edwin O. Excell and Johnson Oatman Jr. "Count Your Blessings," *Hymns of The Church of Jesus Christ of Latter-day Saints* (Salt Lake City: The Church of Jesus Christ of Latter-day Saints, 1985), 241.

6. Jamie Anderson, *MindJournal*, themindsjournal.com/grief-is-love/.

7. *Shadowlands*, DVD, directed by Richard Attenborough (Hollywood, CA: Paramount Home Entertainment, 1993).

CHAPTER 7

Clean Pain versus Dirty Pain

"Therefore, he giveth this promise unto you,
with an immutable covenant that they shall
be fulfilled; and all things wherewith you have
been afflicted shall work together for your
good, and to my name's glory, saith the Lord."

—Doctrine and Covenants 98:3

In 1969, a Swiss psychiatrist named Elisabeth Kübler-Ross presented a widely accepted model for moving through grief in her book *On Death and Dying*. Sometimes referred to as DABDA, the stages she described include denial, anger, bargaining, depression, and acceptance.[1] Using this framework, psychologists, doctors, grief counselors, and others established a general guide to predict human behavior following a traumatic event. For many years, people in grief were expected to follow this prescribed pattern, thinking that once they reached the final stage of acceptance, then their healing would be complete. Dust hands. Move forward. Grief resolved.

Over time, criticism of this model emerged, prompting Dr. Kübler-Ross to refine the model from five to seven stages. To improve the model, she added "shock" as stage one and "testing" between depression and acceptance. While these basic categories are helpful as they showcase the reality that grief is indeed a process, the criticism persisted as many grievers emphasized that true grief is rarely linear or comes in a specific sequential order.

I once saw a meme that showed two tables. One was a professional-looking graph highlighting the traditional stages of grief in a linear DABDA progression. This was juxtaposed next to a homemade graph labeled "My Grief" with DABDA represented in a circle, instead of a line, with sporadic zig-zags crossed back and forth from one stage to another, sometimes bouncing back to the very stage they just left. The message, though intended to be humorous, was still loud and clear—grief is not formulaic, clean, or predictable. Nor is it a one-time, consecutive, step-by-step experience.

It can take time to process heavy emotions. Many people skip stages all together or circle back to repeat certain stages over and over again, even after significant healing has taken place. Sometimes the bereaved can get stuck in a stage of grief such as anger or denial as they are unable or unwilling to move through the process. This is not an indication of weakness, merely of humanness.

For myself, I found that my introductory exposure to the stages of grief was experienced in remarkably short bursts, sometimes one stage occurring almost simultaneously with another. In the aftershock of losing Aiden, my initial reaction was a mixture of shock and denial, quickly followed by depression, bargaining, testing, and finally acceptance—all experienced within a time span of less than thirty minutes. However, anger was the only stage that I never encountered until a completely unrelated incident occurred nearly two years later.

Yet denial was almost instantly present on the morning of Aiden's passing as I wondered if the doctor had made a mistake. Was it possible that the ultrasound machinery had malfunctioned and this was just a final test to see if we really believed in miracles?

When Burke and I were finally left in peace in our labor and delivery room, the first thing on both of our minds was, what about the promise from the priesthood blessing? The "bumpy road full of mental turmoil, anguish, and many difficult decisions to be made" had proved to be prophetic and was fulfilled to the tee. But what about the most important part, the part I thought of as a promise from God? The portion of the blessing that had given me hope, strength, and courage knowing that "in the end, these babies will come whole and healthy."

I had trusted that blessing. I had prayed for and believed we would receive a miracle because of it. Where were my whole and healthy babies? Where was my miracle?

Suddenly, in my state of shock, denial, and bargaining, an idea came to me. In a flash I tried to explain it to Burke. Just a day or two before we had listened to a talk given by our then prophet, Thomas S. Monson, from his most recent general conference address. In his talk, he spoke of a member of The Church of Jesus Christ of Latter-Days Saints, a pilot in the South Pacific during World War II who had been shot down. He and his crew had survived the crash and were floating in a life boat in the wreckage. Three times rescue ships had come within sight but had passed on without seeing them. On the third day, a ship came into view again, but it too passed and was fading out of sight when the Holy Ghost spoke to the man saying, "You have the priesthood. Command the rescuers to pick you up." He did as prompted. "In the name of Jesus Christ and by the power of the priesthood, turnabout and pick us up." Remarkably, the boat turned, came back, and spotted the men who were all saved.[2]

I knew the priesthood was the way we could access the power of God. I believed that if God willed it, we could still have our miracle. As fast as I could, I reminded Burke of this amazing story and then asked, "Burkie, can you do it? Can you call him back? Can you make his spirit return?"

It was a bold request. Burke processed my question for a moment and replied with simple faith, "I can try."

As soon as he said those words, hope rose within me and I was able to stop crying for the first time since Aiden's heartbeat had been found silent. I felt nervous butterflies fluttering around inside, primed to witness the power of God firsthand.

With a surprisingly clear voice and strong hands, Burke began the blessing. After confirming the anointing, he paused for several long moments. In my mind, I waited with bated breath, pleading for the Lord's promised miracle to manifest itself, but for the strength to accept His will and the words that would come regardless.

After swallowing hard, Burke said five words that told me everything I needed to know. "Emily, your son is well." I began to weep again. I knew with those words that Aiden would not be brought back. I knew he was alive, whole and healthy, just as promised, but on the other side of the veil.

Burke continued, "Please know, there is mercy in this." From those words, I knew then that if Aiden had stayed and been delivered that day, he would *not* have been whole and healthy. As the doctors had all warned, his little body had already undergone so much trauma from not receiving the nutrients it needed for so many months, that he would have had intense struggles. I don't know if those challenges would have been physical or mental, or both, and as painful as it was to accept, it was indeed merciful for his spirit to be free from a body that may be full of pain and unimaginable challenges.

I don't remember much more from the blessing, but I know that it helped to bring a spirit of peace and acceptance into the room and our hearts. Once the brother who had helped with the blessing left, Burke and I discussed what had happened, mulling over our questions and concerns, bringing comfort to one another. Rather than giving into the temptation of turning our hearts to stony anger or thoughts of betrayal, pushing us away from our Heavenly Father, we instead turned to Him with pleading, broken hearts in this moment, and despite the sadness, a sense of peace and calm began to enter in. We discussed the reality of the Atonement suffered by our Savior, Jesus Christ. We knew He could take this pain from us. We knew that because of Him, we could see Aiden someday in his whole and perfect state. We knew we could be a forever family as long as we held faithful to our temple covenants that bound us to our son who never walked upon this earth. These eternal truths soothed our aching hearts and brought enormous comfort as the Holy Ghost testified that what we had believed all our lives was, in fact, true. The Spirit was very strong, making that room a holy space, and I fought to cling to the acceptance of what *was*, rather than give in to despair of what could have been.

As we discussed, a thought pierced my heart like a ray of light through a dark cloudy sky. "Burkie," I said, "I think we did have a miracle. It was a miracle that Aiden held on for as long as he did. He must have done it for his brother—for Alan, his twin. He knew that if we had thought he wouldn't be able to hold on, we would have intervened much earlier to save him. He must have fought on until thirty-two weeks so that Alan could have all the time he needed to develop normally."

It rang so true to both of us. We knew in that moment that somehow, Aiden must have had some choice in this matter. We felt strongly that he chose to lay down his own life so his special twin brother could come "whole and healthy" and live for both of them. This was the greatest comfort of all, to think of that twin bond—that remarkable connection of love and blood and spirit—defying all medical data and all logic.

Though I would enter countless rounds of the grief cycle in the coming months and years, our first encounter was incredibly short-lived. The miracle of the Savior's Atonement, with a power that I can hardly comprehend, lifted us out of the dark abyss of our grief and elevated us into the sunlight and peace of the knowledge that we were, in reality, an eternal family.

The tricky thing about grief is that it will never manifest itself in exactly the same way with any two people. Just as no two stories are the same, neither are two sorrowing hearts. Although Burke was by my side throughout the entire ordeal of losing our son, his experience was, in many ways, very different from mine. While I had formed a deep connection with our babies as they grew within me and mourned for our son as though he was already an integral part of our family, Burke's grief was less pronounced. Of course, he loved our son and lamented his loss, but his personality and connection with Aiden were both so different from mine, that his experience with grief manifested in ways that were completely individualized to him.

The symptoms of grief can present themselves in unique ways physically, socially, or spiritually, differing from person to person. Some of the most common symptoms of grief are crying, headaches, difficulty sleeping, questioning the purpose of life or your spiritual beliefs, feelings of detachment, isolation from friends and family, anxiety, fatigue, anger, loss of appetite, and physical aches and pains. In some extreme cases, the intensity of one's sadness can even lead to temporary or perpetual illness. A mourner could experience one, all, or none of these indications of sorrow. Typically, these symptoms will fade over time, which is why the cliché "time heals all wounds" exists.

However, if you find that even with the passage of time you are still having trouble functioning, or if your grief is creating obstacles for you in your everyday life, there are many avenues you can take to begin the healing process. Some bereaved need prescription medications to help them out of a deep depression, onslaughts of anxiety, or even sleeping problems that can come as a result of grief. Others find healing and relief through talk therapy with a counselor, support or bereavement groups, or through discussions with their bishop or Relief Society leaders. Having someone listen to and validate your pain is often essential to sorting through grief. A thoughtful friend, an attentive spouse, or an in-tune family member can make a huge difference for the bereaved by simply allowing them a safe space to express their feelings and thoughts vocally, without fear of judgment.

While talking through pain is a fundamental step in mending our wounds, another coping strategy for heartache is found in creation. Some, like myself, find it therapeutic to write, garden, exercise, paint, or do any number of creative or physical outlets to channel emotions. Taking a quiet walk in the sunshine can be as healing for one individual as composing a song may be for another. When trying to decide which creative outlet will bring you increased peace, it is important to weigh how you will feel at its conclusion. The most powerful activities are those that rejuvenate our bodies, minds, and souls, replenishing us with the essence of hope. These various approaches from Pilates to prose are not meant to be a "cure" for loss but may simply add tools to our belt to help deal with our sadness more effectively.

There is an element of grief called the Dual Process Theory which essentially says that it is healthy to take a break from the labor of grief. Our brains can only grind on for so long before needing respite. Some seek to alleviate the strain on their emotions and minds by numbing out with unhealthy coping strategies such as drinking excessive amounts of alcohol, using drugs to dull the pain, or engaging in other dangerous relationships and activities. Some may find escapism in more tame addictions such as overeating, indulging in too many sweets, binging Netflix series, or online shopping in an attempt to avoid feeling low. While these examples may give us a temporary high, they all have negative consequences. However, certain activities, when done intentionally to help us to "push pause" on the grieving process, can be a healthy release without the adverse side effects. Pastimes such as listening to cheerful music, participating in a hobby, or attending a social event can temporarily alleviate the pressure from the mental and emotional work of sorrow.

As time wears on and the work of grief continues, we may wonder when we will ever get back to "normal". Kübler-Ross said it best when she sympathized, "The reality is that you will grieve forever. You will not 'get over' the loss . . . you will learn to live *with* it. You will heal, and you will rebuild yourself around the loss you have suffered. You will be whole again, but you will never be the same. Nor *should* you be the same, nor would you want to."[3]

Although we may forever be changed by our loss, it is important to eventually begin working toward healing and growth, not only for the sake of our personal physical, mental, and emotional health, but also if we value maintaining and building functional relationships with others. It is possible for our legitimate feelings of sadness to become twisted into a destructive anchor dragging us down and drowning us in the depth of our suffering. We may feel a desire to become reclusive for a time in order to cope with our grief, but in order to build and maintain functional relationships and participate in society, we have to learn how to enter the world again. So, how can someone know when they have crossed over from healthy sadness that is natural and serves us in our mending, to prolonged pain that inhibits healing and growth?

Jody Moore, a prominent life coach and host of a popular podcast, *Better Than Happy*, captivated my attention with her description of a concept she refers to as clean pain versus dirty pain. Jody explains on her website:

Clean pain is a part of life. It is necessary. It helps us grow and heal. Allowing it is important. Resisting it hurts worse than the pain itself. It's the deep sadness you feel after losing a loved one. It's the hurt you feel after being betrayed. It's the fear you feel upon losing a job. It's the disappointment you feel when your plans don't work out. Clean pain almost feels good because it is so cleansing.

Dirty pain is created by your mind. It is not necessary. It does not help. It stops your mind from finding solutions and instead points it in the direction of finding evidence that something is wrong with you, with someone else, with your life or with the world. It is created by thoughts such as: I will never be happy now that my best friend is gone. I am so stupid for not realizing I was being taken advantage of. I should NOT have been let go from that job! I am a horrible person for making that mistake. I'm worried about what COULD go wrong in the future. Dirty pain is minimized by allowing yourself to truly feel clean pain. But all of us create at least some dirty pain, and the majority of the pain we feel in life IS dirty pain.[4]

I wanted to dive deeper into this concept of clean pain versus dirty pain and was thankful Jody agreed to be interviewed to discuss it further. One thing that stuck out to me from our conversation was Jody's reiteration that social science research shows that most people live their lives experiencing fifty percent negative emotion and fifty percent positive emotion. Even when circumstances are changed in ways that most would view as "good" (getting a giant bonus at work), we may feel happier for a time, but generally, we equalize and are presented with the 50/50 once again. Jody explained, "The goal is not to *not* feel pain. We call it clean pain because it's part of that 50/50 , and it's okay to keep those thoughts if you want to. Sometimes, there are situations where we *want* to feel sadness about them, and there is nothing wrong with that."[5]

For example, let's imagine a young newlywed couple who are healthy and strong with the whole world ahead of them. If a tragic accident were to leave the husband paralyzed, his bride would want to feel grief over the loss of his health and the future she had envisioned. The dirty pain enters in when she begins to use words such as "This *shouldn't* have happened" or if she begins placing blame on herself.

Jody spoke of her work as a life coach and specifically her ability to show her clients that all thoughts are optional. "When my client's thoughts are stuck in dirty pain, all I do is show them, look, you're punishing yourself with that thought, and that thought is optional."[6] We can cause harmful dirty pain when we tear ourselves down internally, when we resist what is or attempt to cling to our identity of who we were before a difficult experience. We are all continually in a state of metamorphosis, both subtly and substantially, due to the circumstances of our lives. When we embrace those changes, even if there are growing pains involved, we will have greater success in evolving into a more refined creature than when we resist opportunities for development.

One way that Jody helps her clients discover if they are mentally in a space of clean pain or dirty pain is by having them write down their story as if it were the headline for a newspaper. Let's take that same imaginary newlywed couple again by way of example. If the title the young wife chooses for her story is "Woman's Husband Has Terrible Accident that Ruins Their Life," then every point in the article will be structured to support that pessimistic lens. If the young woman believes her self-imposed title is true, she will begin looking for—and finding!—evidence to support that narrative. Her focus will be a negative orientation, and she will fixate on the awful elements this ordeal has brought into their lives. Obviously, the result of these negative thoughts will be heavy "dirty pain" as the young wife carries guilt and shame on top of the natural "clean pain" from the situation.

However, if the young woman instead chooses to believe that this hardship was always supposed to happen, the revised title might read, "Woman's Husband Has Terrible Accident and They Remain Joyful." Think of the vastly different perspective she will develop if looking at her husband's accident from that angle. Instead of layering herself with more pain from shame and guilt, she is free now to focus on the positive elements of their story. Perhaps due to his accident, her husband chooses another career path that brings him greater fulfillment in life. Maybe this incident solidifies their love for one another in a way that never could have happened otherwise. Though there still may be clean pain from the reality that being wheelchair-bound will dramatically change their lives, the woman will be in a much better space to help her husband and herself through this misfortune than she would otherwise be able to while consumed with the dirty pain.

Jody explained, "We get to write our own book! We can change the ending. If we find we are unhappy with the story, we have the power. We don't need to deny that hard things happened, but we *can* change the lens it if we want to."[7] Though we cannot control the issues that may arise in our life, we do have the privilege and responsibility to determine how we will respond to them. "Faith, Hope, and Courage" is always an option for our book's title. Many of the women I interviewed chose just that.

Kelsea

Kelsea is a fantastic example of someone who was able to examine her thoughts to change her perspective about a challenge. When her oldest son, Ty, was just three years old, he taught himself to read. Soon after, Kelsea went to get Ty from his room after nap time. Confused, she found that he had taken a pencil and drawn hundreds of tick marks in a pattern around the bedroom walls and had begun making a second row by the time she discovered him. In kindergarten, he attempted to shove a child into another while standing in a line so he could observe a "domino effect."

"At first, I didn't know how much of his behavior I should chalk up to being five or just because he was a rambunctious little boy. But he was starting to get sent to the principal's office and having a hard time making friends. The more I saw his obsession with patterns and his inability to stay focused on simple tasks like getting dressed, I began to realize that his brain just did not work the same as most people."

For five more years Kelsea and her husband struggled with Ty's behavioral and cognitive differences until they were able to get him officially diagnosed with Autism Spectrum Disorder. Initially, Kelsea mourned the loss of a future she had imagined for Ty, especially as she watched the aversion other children sometimes had to his odd behavior and the effect it had on his self-esteem. She wondered if he would ever have "normal" relationships or be able to excel in school.

"I won't lie that it's been frustrating and painful to be on this journey with Ty and watch him struggle. It has only been in the last year that I feel like I have had a radical change of thought. Ty's situation is no longer a 'sorrow' to me. It's certainly a challenge, but I have come to view Ty's brain as simply a remapping. Autism should not be looked at as a disability; it was just the way he was born. We see the rising rates of children with autism and I choose to think, 'What if their brains are being remapped for a reason? What if there are things that they need their senses to be turned off to or zoned in on so that Heavenly Father can use their unique gifts in some special way?' If Ty focuses on the things that he's interested in rather than on kids not being nice to him, he excels. And now, when I meet other families who are going through something similar, I feel like I can be an advocate, I can be a voice, I can be a mentor to help them realize that their child has been given a gift rather than a curse."

Kelsea freed herself from sorrow when she let go of the dirty pain associated with Ty's autism. Although initially she would have preferred for his brain to function similar to her own so she would have a better understanding of how to nurture and teach him, Kelsea realized that it was harmful to herself and her son to mourn what "should have been." Once she relinquished a desire for something that would never be and instead focused on the opportunities and lessons learned from what *was* and *is*, she was able to find peace.

Marsha

Marsha and Dave watch the graceful circling of the falcon, their breath held in anticipation. Without a hint, the bird plummets rocket-like toward the earth below. The two spectate in awe, exhilarated by the natural air show as the falcon pulls up from his fantastic dive at the last possible moment, his prey clutched helplessly in his sharp talons.

Falconry has become a symbol of unity for the couple, a hobby that draws them together, showing how far they have come in their relationship. Not long ago, the two struggled to find a single common interest. For many years, Marsha had been at war with her husband. Although they loved one another fiercely, there was a constant, festering wound in their relationship. Whenever it looked as though things were finally healing, Dave would have another relapse with his substance abuse addictions, causing him to fall in and out of church activity.

"We've been married for fifty years now, and all that time Dave has never really made up his mind whether or not he was 'all in' with the gospel. But when I look back on his history, it makes sense why his addictions have always had such a strong hold on him. He started smoking at eleven and quit so he could serve a mission, but really it was just a temporary fix since he picked it right back up when he returned. For a while, when we were newlyweds, we made some dumb choices. I finally decided that the way we were living was not the way I wanted our children to be raised. I made up my mind then and there that this was it for me. I was going to give my everything to the gospel, and from that point on, I always have."

For decades Marsha kept nurturing the dream that Dave would one day wake up free from his addictions and be the man she knew he had the potential to be inside. However, as time went on, she finally realized something. "Every time I was disappointed because he did things I didn't want him to do, I realized I was driving a wedge further and further between us. I finally decided that, just like I had made up my mind to give everything to the Lord, I could also make up my mind to just love Dave for who he is."

Once Marsha changed her perspective, she freed herself from the dirty pain of wanting her life to look a certain way. Instead, she began noticing the good in her husband and in her children, which resulted in an increase of love and a decrease in criticism. Even when her family didn't make the decisions she wanted them to make, she could now acknowledge the things they did well and the ways they were trying. "I've discovered that my happiness and love of the gospel are not contingent on the agency of others. I wish I had realized this secret years ago, but I'm glad that I have that knowledge now. It's a much happier way to live."

Hannah

It was an ordinary Sabbath day. Hannah sat down to a bountiful homemade Sunday dinner roast with her former Primary president mother, valiant priesthood father, and three of five sisters who still lived at home. Sure, the sisters squabbled from time to time, but in Hannah's fourteen-year-old mind, they were happy. A pretty-near-perfect family. After stuffing themselves on the delicious dinner, the girls went back to their various Sunday lounge activities, content and at peace. A couple of hours passed before anything odd was noted.

"Where's Mom?" a daughter asked.

"Around," another sister replied.

That seemingly ordinary Sunday dinner turned out to be the last time Hannah saw her mother for over a year. She simply packed a bag, shut the door quietly, and left. She left it all. Her husband. Her daughters. Her picture-perfect life.

"I should have realized at the time that she must have been hurting for a long time. That she was dealing with her demons and depression that none of us had ever even fathomed she was carrying. I mean, she was the model mother. She hand-made all of our clothes, she volunteered in our classrooms, she served without complaint. But as a teenager, I just couldn't see how this could be anyone's fault but mine. I spent years trying to hide from that pain. I distracted myself with dance and friends and boys and being rebellious—anything to keep me busy, to keep me from feeling."

But no matter how busy Hannah tried to stay, there was always the haunting, aching knowledge that her mother had left them. She had left *her*.

* * *

Just like the women above, I have experienced elements of both clean and dirty pain as I have worked through my grief. When I look back and examine my thoughts after losing Aiden, I can point to a definitive moment where I had to choose one versus the other. My clean pain could be described as the deep pain I felt as a mother losing the ability to raise my son in this life. The dirty pain came when my brain offered me these excruciating thoughts: My son died *because* of me. If I were a better mother, if I had more faith, if I had only prayed more, he would be here now.

If I could go back, I would have stopped myself when these toxic thoughts first arrived on the scene. I would have voiced them and brought them out of the dark place in the back of my mind where they festered in fear and shame. If I could do it again, I would have named these thoughts for what they were—destructive tools of the adversary. But because I was afraid of these thoughts, I shoved them back in a closet in my mind and hoped that they would disappear. But dirty pain doesn't dissipate on its own. Instead, those damaging thoughts would sneak out at unexpected times, gaining strength each time I found "evidence" to support their lies.

A few weeks after we lost Aiden, we learned that a co-worker of Burke's was also pregnant with identical twins, and surprisingly, their babies ended up with almost the same unusual medical issues our boys had struggled with. It was unnerving to me to hear about their challenges from a distance, to feel so connected to their story and yet so helpless. Knowing the tragic way our situation had turned out, we prayed that they would be spared a similar fate and waited for news.

Thankfully, in the case of this sweet family, their pleadings were answered in an ideal way with both babies arriving early, but healthy and beautifully developed. I was relieved and happy for them, but I would be lying if I didn't admit that my heart felt a tiny twinge of pain at the news.

The lie my brain had planted months before reared its ugly head, telling me this other mother must have been more righteous than me, more patient, more loving. Both of her babies came because she must have passed the same test that I had failed. Again, if I had spoken these words out loud, I would have heard the false ring, but as sociology researcher Brené Brown has said, "Shame thrives in secrecy,"[8] and so did my dirty pain.

Shortly after the birth of the coworker's treasured twins, I met the aunt of this new mother and rejoiced with her in the safe arrival of the babies. She rightly celebrated their miraculous birth and said with conviction, "You know, one or both of those babies should have passed away. It was a miracle! I know that things would have turned out differently if it hadn't been for the prayers on those babies' behalf. I know it's because our family fasted and had enough faith that they were saved!"

I don't know how I excused myself from that conversation without shattering into a million pieces. All my darkest thoughts seemed to be confirmed in that moment. They had enough faith, and their babies were healed, which obviously meant that (since I knew how strong the faith of all of our support network had been), I was the weak link. Somehow, I had been found lacking. My self-composed title for our circumstance could have read at that moment, "Woman Loses Baby Because She Didn't Have Enough Faith."

This was the height of my dirty pain. I didn't realize at the time, but I was at the pinnacle of my Victimhood, nearly ready to progress in my Growth Through Grief to Phase Two: Survivor.

ENDNOTES

1. Christina Gregory, PhD, "The Five Stages of Grief—An Examination of the Kubler-Ross Model," psycom.net/depression.central.grief.html.
2. Thomas S. Monson, "A Sacred Trust," churchofjesuschrist.org/study/general-conference/2016/04/a-sacred-trust?lang=eng, April 2016.
3. Elisabeth Kubler-Ross, *On Grief and Grieving: Finding the Meaning of Grief Through the Five Stages of Loss* (Scribner, 2005).
4. Jody Moore, "Is Your Pain Clean or Dirty?" jodymoore.com/pain-clean-dirty/.
5. Judy Moore, personal interview with Emily Adams via Zoom, January 15, 2020.
6. Ibid.
7. Ibid.
8. Brene Brown (@BreneBrown). 2019. Twitter post, May 8, 2019. twitter.com/BreneBrown/status/1126301981751029760.

CHAPTER 8

What Now?

Phase 2: Survivor

"And now, my sons, remember, remember that it is upon the rock of our Redeemer, who is Christ, the Son of God, that ye must build your foundation; that when the devil shall send forth his mighty winds, yea, his shafts in the whirlwind, yea, when all his hail and his mighty storm shall beat upon you, it shall have no power over you to drag you down to the gulf of misery and endless wo, because of the rock upon which ye are built, which is a sure foundation, a foundation whereon if men build they cannot fall."

—Helaman 5:12

In 1946, just one year after the conclusion of the atrocities of the Holocaust during World War II, Viktor Frankl published a book entitled *Man's Search for Meaning*, detailing his horrific experiences as a prisoner in a Nazi concentration camp. I find it shocking that he had the ability to write about and dissect this horrific nightmare so soon after his liberation.

One issue that Frankl wrestled with in this initial book, and on into the many books that would follow in later years, was the conundrum of meaning. Was it just random bad luck that he was dragged into the hellish horror of the Holocaust, or could it be possible that there was omniscient reasoning behind it all? Frankl had an agonizing battle with this unsolvable question. In the end, he decided there was no way to know as he could not prove a position definitively either way. Essentially, he decided that when faced with trials, we have two options. We can either see it as random, or we can look for a deeper purpose. When Frankl decided to deliberately choose to view the circumstances of his life as meaningful, he found that he handled the trauma of his memories more effectively. He discovered that these experiences didn't hurt him as much knowing it could serve him or others in some way. With powerful insight Frankl said, "Suffering ceases to be suffering at the moment it finds a meaning."[1]

When it comes to the sorrow in our lives, there comes a time we have to ask ourselves, "What will I do with this pain?" A sense of deeper healing is achieved when we can view our difficulty with a level of objectivity. When we can step back and see the lessons learned from our trials, and the possible meaning behind it, we have transitioned into a Survivor.

A Survivor has come to a sense of peace about their sorrow. This is the place where we begin to find answers to the *why* questions we asked in the first phase of Victimhood. The *why* might not be spelled out directly for us, but rather may gain the purpose we choose to assign it. Remember—we are writing our story, and we get to decide what we will make of this challenge. Jody Moore taught me in our interview, "When you take accountability for the way you think about yourself and your story, when you take ownership for your situation—that's what moves you out of Victimhood."

You've probably heard some variation of the expression, "You can become bitter or you can become better," and in many ways, what we *do* with our trials is that simple. You can choose to take what has been dealt to you in this life and allow it to make you a better person because of it or let it hold you back. This is not something fate appoints, but rather, it is an intentional choice. Some people have mindsets that are naturally inclined toward pessimism or optimism, while others are trained to think positively or negatively due to the way they were raised.

A key element to overcoming Victim mindset and transitioning into a Survivor is being able to cultivate an attitude of gratitude. For some, that expression may elicit a cringe as they picture Disney's happy-go lucky Pollyanna from the 1960s. To attempt to apply Polly-anna's sunny optimism to a history of abuse sounds absurd. A person need not paste on a false perma-smile and pretend they are happy about the horrible events in their lives in order to cultivate gratitude. We need not to be thankful for a difficult challenge. Instead we can look for the lessons learned *because* of that challenge and instead find gratitude in the wisdom gained.

My parents taught me that there is always purpose to be found in our circumstances. They taught me the art of gratitude. In the eve-nings we gathered for dinner, Mom and Dad seated as equal partners at opposite heads of our creaky oak table. Eight blue-eyed children squished four to a bench on either side as we practiced giving thanks. While we ate, Mom or Dad would often start by calling on a child and asking, "What did you feel grateful for today, Elijah?" Winding around the table, each would have the opportunity to share, and I always felt eager to come up with something unique to add to the mix.

This precedence of expressing gratitude was especially palpable each year during our family's special "Talking Stick" tradition. The Talking Stick is a Native American custom my father had learned from a client in his psychology practice and adopted in our home. The stick was a worn walking staff, adorned with feathers dangling from leather cords. The ritual began with the silent passing of the stick from one family member to the next while looking around the circle into the eyes of each person present, acknowledging the worth of their spirit. As children, and especially as teens, we suppressed laughter in our dis-comfort with the quietude, making small jokes by bulging our eyes at one another or raising dramatic eyebrows. Once one grand circle had been completed, all speech was prohibited unless you were the one holding the stick. The speaker often intensely twisted the cords and absentmindedly stroked the feathers while sharing the poignant lessons they had amassed that year.

Besides the occasional giggle or sniffle elicited in reaction to the speaker's words, our family of ten surprisingly complied with this rev-erent tradition. The silence alone was a rarity from such an outspo-ken tribe. Still, the tangible spirit working to unite our hearts as one was the foundation for future family miracles yet unseen. Typically, I learned more in that hour or two of sharing of the inner struggles, growth, and testimony my siblings had experienced that year than I had ever guessed they had been involved in while sharing the same roof with them day in and day out.

When it was my father's turn, he would invariably comment at some point how yet another year had come and gone, and we continued to be blessed as a family. In a vague way, I remember perceiving an underlying tremor of stress when he would make these comments, as if he feared any day our blessings would run out, that the earth would quake, rattling our carefully maintained foundation. He would often say while shaking his head with disbelief, "I just don't know how long we can prolong being so blessed, but oh, how grateful I am to our Heavenly Father that we continue to be."

Year after year, the message remained the same.

When I was pregnant with our oldest daughter, the well of good fortune at last "dried up" for our family. My iron man father, who had never missed a day of work in his life due to illness, was diagnosed with stage 4 chronic lymphocytic leukemia (CLL) the week before Thanksgiving. This was it. The tragedy we had feared would come. And yet, when we sat down for a family meeting at Christmas and passed the beloved Talking Stick, Dad, pale and weak from chemotherapy, repeated the same message of gratitude he had always conveyed: "I just don't know how long we can keep being so blessed, but oh, how grateful I am that we continue to be!" Even with a funeral plan in hand, Dad continued to count his blessings.

My father once wrote, "The truth is not so much about finding faith in self or in others, but faith that something positive can come of even the most challenging situation: that the process of life is good, even when bad things happen to decent people."[2] Dad's near-immediate acceptance of his unexpected health challenges and complete faith in Heavenly Father's plan was a remarkable example to my family at a time when we were all reeling from shock, each person coming to terms with the possibility of losing the cherished patriarch of our home to cancer. As we worked through our sorrow, Dad's serenity had a profound influence, bringing a greater sense of unity, faith, and gratitude to the whole family.

For some, like my father, the transition from Victim to Survivor is almost instantaneous. For others, their internal battle to move from one phase to another may take years. While for another subset, they may vacillate between feelings of peace and turmoil centered on the same challenge.

Often an individual is ready to move forward in their grief but may hold themselves back, feeling ashamed of "forgetting" their sorrow. For example, when we have lost a loved one, we may notice ourselves laughing or feeling happy and instantly try to squash those good feelings. We may think that if we're not having the intense emotions of suffering all the time, then maybe we aren't showing how deeply we miss our departed one. Perhaps we make it mean that maybe we didn't love them enough.

This was one of the greatest challenges for me following the twins' birth. In the hospital, I was both mourning *and* simultaneously rejoicing. I felt sick with grief as I held Aiden's still, cold form in one arm, and yet overflowing with love as I cuddled Alan's warm body to me in the other arm. It was an exhausting emotional seesaw and one that I am still seeking to balance, especially when we hit milestones. When we celebrate the twins' birthday, I snap pictures and watch with delight as Alan opens presents and tastes his cake, my smile genuine and full of love. However, five minutes later I could be hiding in a closet, sobbing into my clothes to muffle the sound as I imagine how different this day would be if both boys were here playing with new trucks side by side, their identical grins a mile wide. How I long for mischievous carbon copy laughter making a mess of the wrapping paper, the way I hear other "twin-nadoes" do. This life with our twinless twin is a constant hybrid of bittersweet.

This returns us to Jody Moore's 50/50 rule, where the majority of the population experiences positive emotion 50 percent of the time and negative emotion 50 percent of the time. At our core, all mankind wants the same things: as much love and happiness available with as little pain and suffering as possible.

In the Book of Mormon, the most frequently repeated line is "it came to pass," not "it came to stay." Just like Jody's 50/50 rule, nothing good or bad lasts forever in this life. Youth, health, and beauty will fade. Friendships will evolve. Children will grow up. This is especially good news for those of us who are still up with babies and dying the slow death of the sleep-deprived. Eventually those children *will* learn how to sleep, and someday they will be teenagers who are impossible to wake. There are wonderful days ahead and hard days too, but neither will be around permanently. Consequently, we should try our best to enjoy the good times more fully when they are here and put less emphasis on the bad times when they arrive on the scene.

A productive thought that I learned from Jody that may help with an individual's progression to Survivor is this: nothing in our life happens *to* us, it all happens *for* us. Pondering this statement may lead to the beneficial question posed by all who are ready to transition into Survivors: "What can I learn from this?" Taking ownership of our thoughts regarding our trials, and accountability for what we make of them, is a catalyst for moving forward. Many of my interviewees could recall examples of their own evolutions of thought that led them from the Victim phase on to Survivor.

Shanette

"When I served my mission in Spain many years ago, one of our sister missionaries prayed for more patience, walked out the door, and fell and broke her leg!" At first, Shanette wondered how such a terrible thing could happen until she realized the experience was meant to teach the missionary that very thing—more patience. "Ever since that vicarious experience, I just thought, okay, so everything I go through is a learning process, so when I am going through a hard time if I can just start thinking, 'what am I going to learn from this?' Is it this? Is it that? Almost like I'm searching for the lesson no matter what situation I'm in. In some ways, I think, the faster I can learn the lesson, the faster I can get out of this class, and the trial can end!"

One "class" that was extremely unpleasant for Shanette was watching as her son's friends left on missions while her son drifted further away from the gospel and chose to follow a different path. As has been her habit since her mission, Shanette instantly began searching for the lesson, trying to find a way to learn what she needed to so she could get him on a mission and make it all better.

"It took me a little while before I finally realized that the lesson was not so much about making this situation go away. I cannot change him. He has his agency, and that is how God designed this plan. I cannot *make* him have the testimony I have. The thing I needed to learn was how to love my child unconditionally, even if he doesn't choose the path I want him to. Once I recognized that, I could stop feeling so much sadness and just work on loving him better."

Meranda

Meranda was a victim in every sense of the word. The sorrow of her life stemmed from the sexual, physical, and emotional abuse she experienced as a child in a dysfunctional home. As a young girl, she was made to believe the destructive lie that she was ugly and worthless. For many years, she was plagued with timidity and self-doubt after constantly being put down by those who were supposed to love her most. But as time went on, an innate strength began to rise up within her until she was at last able to say, "No more." No to those who had stood back and neglected her. No to those who had known she was suffering and done nothing to intervene. And especially no to her abusers.

It took many years for Meranda to learn how to completely extricate herself from those toxic relationships, but over time she began to forge a new path for herself. As she gained confidence, she took her healing into her own hands and began to change the way she saw herself by changing her thoughts. Instead of believing the harmful story that she was unattractive and mediocre, Meranda defied this distortion and began to contract out as a model, choosing to believe that she was beautiful and worthy—inside and out. After working with a counselor who could help her heal from the scars of her past, she returned to her university studies and studied psychology in hopes of gaining the training necessary to help others heal as she had.

"Sometimes trees get struck by lightning. Although I didn't deserve the treatment I received, it still happened. I feel like a tree that has been struck, and now I have this big split down the middle. But sometimes, against all odds, half of the tree recovers and grows back. And I feel like that's what is happening now. That's the best way I can try to compare it."

Amy

Amy had promised her father that she would look after Mother if the time ever came that he couldn't be there to do it anymore. That time had come, and Amy wasn't one to break a promise. Perhaps it began with what Amy termed "dutiful daughter syndrome," as her two brothers followed their paths away from home, leaving the heavy weight of caring for their struggling mother solely on Amy's shoulders. However, when the choices came—jobs and men and dreams—one by one she turned them down. She chose Mother. "I made my peace with it. I wasn't disappointed. I had to give up a lot of my own desires."

When she looked back over her life, Amy felt as though God's unseen hand had been training her all her life to be a caretaker. Instead of being bitter about giving up the traditional path of marriage and family, Amy chose to be content with her journey. "I don't feel that I gave up anything. I really didn't. I got to spend time with a wonderful, wonderful woman. And we were real good at taking care of each other. Some will never know what a privilege it is to care for a parent like that. Our lives were completely intertwined."

Donna

As a girl, every type of abuse imaginable was a near-constant horror in Donna's life. She woke up in the morning afraid of what each day would bring. There was no support system to help her through it, no extended family or neighbors or church. "I was raised with no concept of religion," she said. "None."

At one point in our interview, in complete disbelief of the multitude of trials *one* woman alone had seen in her life, I asked her what had helped her to manage it all. Donna paused for a moment, then put her hand to her mouth as she exclaimed, "You know, until this very moment, I had forgotten a memory that was very dear to me."

Donna went on to describe, "When I was a child, I would often go to bed at night afraid. I was afraid of my step-father and what he might do to me. But when I was a very little girl, I began to have a reoccurring dream. I know I had it a lot, but I seemed to have it most nights after something traumatic had happened. In my dream, I was a beautiful princess, and I just knew that I was someone special. Everything was beautiful, and clean, and bright. I remember feeling so safe. I remember knowing that my father was a king and that he loved me more than I could ever fathom. When I would wake up, I always woke up happy. It was like I just knew that somewhere, somebody loved me, and I would walk around with like this bubble around me, like that dream was protecting me."

As Donna aged, she forgot about the dream. She spent years "looking for love in all the wrong places." As an adult, after two messy divorces, Donna moved to another state where she was introduced to the missionaries. "I remember when they told me for the first time about Heavenly Father and I heard, 'I Am a Child of God.' It was then that I remembered my childhood dream for the first time in literally decades. And I suddenly realized that even though I had so many hard things happen to me, that I really did have a Father, a Heavenly King who loved me. Even though I didn't know anything about God or Jesus or even faith at the time, He hadn't forgotten me. He sent me that dream, that feeling of being loved and safe almost like a little clue or like a love note so that I could know that I wasn't alone."

Tracie

Tracie's family became a running joke in their small town. After a series of bad luck resulted in hospital visits, accidents, and challenges that plagued her family throughout her teenage years, everyone teased that they couldn't catch a break. However, her parents were the kind of people who could keep a sunny outlook no matter the weather. "We were never victims," Tracie said. "My parents taught me why we're here and that challenges are just challenges. I think they were okay with the fact that life wasn't always perfect. That you have hard times, and it's okay to cry, and it's okay to be upset, and it's okay to wonder why things happen. But you also have to realize that just because bad things or hard things happen doesn't mean that God isn't there or that he doesn't love you."

This ability to accept life's challenges would be put to the ultimate test when Tracie was sixteen. "I remember hugging my dad that morning before school and looking down at his shoes. That seems like such a weird thing to remember, but whenever I think back on that day, I see those shoes. I had this feeling that something bad was going to happen to someone in my family, so I would always give everyone hugs before we left and say, 'I love you.' And I'm so glad I did, because I got to tell him that one last time."

Later that morning, Tracie's dad was killed in a car accident. It was a terrible loss for the family and the whole community, where her father had been a pillar of strength to so many. Tracie came home from school to a house packed with people. There was no opportunity to mourn privately. Her mother took out her planner, systematically making phone call after phone call to alert their loved ones. The whole atmosphere was so strange, the constant flow of well-meaning people so exhausting. Tracie at last escaped to her bedroom. She kneeled at her bed and prayed to Heavenly Father.

"I remember I was heartbroken, but I knew that God would be the one to help me through it. I told Him I didn't know why this had happened. I asked Him to help us get through it. But the thing that I remember most about that prayer was asking God to please give my dad a hug for me since I couldn't anymore."

Several months later, her heart still broken, Tracie felt the weight of the patriarch's hands settle onto her head. Her dad had encouraged her to get her patriarchal blessing. Though it was too late to have her dad there in body, she hoped he would be with her in spirit. As the patriarch prayed, emotions flowed freely from everyone in the room as he spoke about her father's passing. He talked of God having a purpose in calling her father home, that He knew it would be terrible and tragic for their family, but that he was well and happy, and he was preparing a home for them when their time came. He told her to be comforted in that knowledge.

"And I was! It always has been a great comfort me to know that he's watching over me and that he's there."

The more Tracie has learned to focus on the promise that there was a purpose for her father's passing and to look for the blessings that have come from her trials, the more peace and joy she has been able to obtain in her life.

* * *

I found this to be true in my own life as I navigated a forest of grief after we lost Aiden. When I focused on all we had lost, a weight would settle on my chest, constricting my breathing, and send my thoughts down a bleak spiral toward depression. However, if I could catch myself and change gears, I would stop my brain before it could spin out, and ask myself, "What would be the purpose of Aiden's short life if it brought only sorrow?"

In the hospital after we had learned Aiden had passed, I felt blessed by a sacred experience that gave me a brief glimpse at what my boy looked like, not as an infant but as an adult. It was as if I could see this handsome, blond-haired young man who looked so much like his daddy. He was grinning at me and radiating a sense of joy, confidence, and total peace with the fact that he had been given a different mortal experience than the one I so desperately wanted for him. I don't know quite how to describe it, but I had the impression that although Aiden's spirit was there with us for a short time after passing through the veil, he would not always be "right there." I felt that he was needed on the other side for a purpose and that he was going to be busy with his tasks, just as we were busy with our responsibilities on earth. He would be here when we needed him most, but he had work to do as well.

On the day we learned Aiden was gone, we were discharged from the hospital and returned to my sister Cassie's home, where she and my mother were caring for our two girls. It was such a challenge to attempt to explain to our young daughters why I was still pregnant instead of bringing home their baby brothers whom they had been so excited to meet. Children have such a difficult time processing the reality of death, and it was gut-wrenching to watch our oldest daughter as she tried to make sense of what we were saying: little brother Aiden's heart hadn't been strong enough, and he had died before we could take the twins out safely. Brother Alan was safe and would have more time to grow now until my body went into labor on its own. We reminded the girls that we were a forever family and that Aiden was still a part of our family, even if he couldn't be with us at this time.

It just so happened to be a Monday night, so my sister Cassie prepared a memorable family home evening lesson for her children and mine. Placing a picture of Jesus Christ on the floor, Cassie instructed all of us to stand in a circle surrounding the picture. Taking a home-drawn arrow, she pointed outward and asked us to all move away from the picture. She asked the children to observe how, when they moved away from Christ, they also were distanced from their loved ones. Next, she pointed the arrow toward the center of the circle and asked us all to "draw near unto Christ." The kids giggled as the circle shrank until we were standing shoulder to shoulder, side by side.

"Do you see?" Cassie asked my girls and their cousins. "The closer we move to Christ, the closer we are to each other. And when we aim for Him, we are also aiming for Aiden, so we'll be able to feel closer to him too."

Cassie's simple demonstration inspired our new family motto: Aim for Aiden. That small expression helped to solidify my conviction to follow Jesus Christ. I had always hoped to live worthy to return to Christ's presence in the life to come, but recognizing that Aiden was already pure enough to be in His company is an extra motivation to live my life in such a way that I can be with my Savior and my son someday.

ENDNOTES

1. Viktor Frankl, *Man's Search for Meaning* (Newark: Audible, 2017). Audiobook.
2. David Bush, *Why Buy the Lie*, unpublished manuscript.

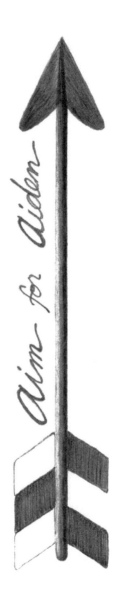

Aim for Aiden

CHAPTER 9

A Man of Sorrows

"He is despised and rejected of men; a man of sorrows, and acquainted with grief; and we hid as it were our faces from him; he was despised, and we esteemed him not. Surely he has borne our griefs, and carried our sorrows."

—Mosiah 14:3–6

In chapter 4, we discussed five categories of suffering as taught by Elder Hales. However, there is one more classification that deserves a discussion all on its own. Elder Hales explained, "The sixth category should remain distinct and separate from the rest as it is a realm of suffering beyond our mortal ability to enter into or for our finite minds to comprehend. Only one individual qualifies."[1]

This individual, of course, is our Savior, Jesus Christ, whose suffering and atoning sacrifice was the most important event in the history of the world. Though we may traverse through one or all of the former five categories of pain and suffering in this life, it is only through category number six, through the Atonement of our Redeemer, the Lord Jesus Christ, that we can be healed from all other sorrows.

Though others may have experienced similar grief to our own and may empathize deeply, the truth is that no other human being can ever fully understand your life, heart, mind, and sorrows as thoroughly and perfectly as Jesus does. The prophet Alma taught, "And [Christ] shall go forth suffering pains and afflictions and temptations of every kind . . . he will take upon him the pains and sicknesses of his people . . . that his bowels may be filled with mercy . . . that he may know according to the flesh how to succor his people according to their infirmities" (Alma 7:11–12).

We have explored several strategies we can utilize to assist us to rise above the grief that accompanies our trials. While these tools can be effective and useful, the only way to achieve a complete metamorphosis from Victim to Survivor in both mind and soul is by fully embracing the gift of the Atonement of Christ. Sister Jean B. Bingham shared, "No matter what we have suffered, He is the source of healing. . . . We must come unto Him and allow Him to work His miracles."[2]

It truly is a miracle when His love transforms the trauma experienced by a Victim into the strength and confidence of a Survivor. He is the Transformer, the Healer, the Restorer, the Mender, the Fixer. Echoing Sister Bingham, Elder Dale G. Renlund taught, "The Savior loves to *restore* what you cannot restore; He loves to *heal* wounds you cannot heal; He loves to *fix* what has been irreparably broken; He *compensates* for any unfairness inflicted on you; and He *loves* to permanently mend even shattered hearts."[3]

When we are staring at the shards of our life, blown to bits by the sheer force of our conflicts, the thought of *anyone* coming along and somehow putting back these obliterated pieces may seem like a fantasy. We may desire to utilize the incomprehensible glue of Christ's Atonement to mend us but are perhaps uncertain how to do so or doubtful if it is even possible. Scores of books have been written and talks given on the complexity and yet beautiful simplicity of the power of Christ's Atonement. Religious scholars have spent decades studying the sophistication of this theology, and yet it is plain enough that a child can grasp its importance.

In The Church of Jesus Christ of Latter-day Saints, often one of the first symbols a child is taught is that Christ's Atonement has the power to take sins red as scarlet and transform them into whiteness as pure as snow. I remember hearing in Primary basic stories such as a young boy hitting a baseball through a window and learning the importance of using the power of Christ's Atonement for repentance and restitution.

As a teen, we were informed in Sunday School that when we have distanced ourselves from God through willful disobedience, praying for forgiveness through Christ's Atonement could cleanse us and bring us back into alignment with our Heavenly Father. However, being a naturally cheerful person and living a life of relative peace in my youth, I may not have paid attention when we were instructed on how Christ's Atonement can be applied to in the case of our sorrows and challenges.

It was not until losing Aiden that I was in sudden and serious need of the healing effects of the Savior's atoning capacity to cure suffering. I wanted to apply that power, but I didn't quite know which key would unlock the door and allow access. While seeking to understand this potential strength, I simply kept on doing the things that I knew led to comfort and revelation in the past, namely the basics: praying, reading my scriptures, studying general conference talks, and attending the temple.

One day, I was reading the scriptures while being weighed down by a sense of shame that my grief continued to persist so strongly. As I read, I came upon a verse that grabbed my full attention: "He is despised and rejected of men; *a man of sorrows, and acquainted with grief;* and we hid as it were our faces from him; he was despised and we esteemed him not" (Mosiah 14:3, emphasis added).

I know I had read that passage many times before, but in light of my guilt over my grief, this information hit me as new and astounding. If Jesus Christ, the very Son of God, was intimately acquainted with grief and sorrow, did that mean those feelings did not equate imperfection? I believed with all my heart that Christ was without blemish, and I would never judge *Him* for experiencing sorrow. So why would I judge myself so harshly? I suppose I'd assumed that as a perfect being, He could let adversity roll off His back and not allow it to affect Him. But does perfection mean not letting words and experiences hurt us? Or does it just mean not permitting them to dull our faith and distance us from our Heavenly Father?

I pondered further. What kind of incidents had arisen in Christ's life prior to Gethsemane that could make Him feel sorrow? If He was "well acquainted with grief," it sounded to me as though He had dealt with more than His fair share of hardships and trials. I dove into the scriptures, looking for further evidence of examples of the Savior's familiarity with grief.

We know that Jesus's mortal body was just like ours, subject to all manner of disease and infirmities. It's strange to think of the man who walked on water sneezing from a head cold or dealing with the complexities of mortal relationships. In the scriptures, we learn that members of His own family did not accept Him as the Messiah (see John 7:5). Villagers who knew him well from His hometown of Nazareth attempted to take His life (see Luke 4:16–3). Friends betrayed Him, denied knowing Him (see Luke 22:48, 54–62), and in the end all forsook Him (see Matthew 26:56). At the death of his friend Lazarus, we read that Jesus wept. He mourned alongside Mary and Martha, empathizing with them despite His knowledge that He would momentarily raise Lazarus from the dead (see John 11:1–46).

If Jesus gave Himself time to grieve a loved one, shouldn't I?

The morning we learned Aiden had passed, I knew the intensity of my pain was so much more than just disappointment or sadness. This was an agony I had never encountered. For the first time in my life, I understood why pain of this magnitude is often described as a gaping hole or wound in your heart. The physical pressure on my chest was so intense, it quite literally felt like my heart was breaking.

The following day, in a quiet moment, Burke and I sat down together when suddenly our loss hit me again with torrential force, and I began to weep with the same abandonment as I had at the hospital. This was real. My baby boy's tiny heart had stopped beating while his brother's beat on. I was no longer going to be raising identical twins, side by side. I was still pregnant. This horrible journey was not yet over. How long did I have until his little body would begin to deteriorate within me? Would I ever get to see Aiden's form and hold him in my arms? How was this affecting his brother, Alan, still growing inside?

The questions and doubts I thought I had settled in the hospital began to churn around like a raging storm within as yet another grief cycle began with another round of shock, denial, and depression. The walls were closing in on me. I needed to do something to regain footing.

I asked Burke to pray for us, and he offered a heartfelt appeal while holding me tightly in his arms, the tears soaking his shirt. After he closed the prayer, he tenderly stroked my head, took a deep breath, and said, "This is where the rubber hits the road, Em. Do we believe the gospel, or don't we?"

I asked myself the same question. Did I believe? Did I truly believe that my son's spirit lived on? That his little life had a purpose, though he had never drawn a breath? That our temple covenants were real and eternally binding? It didn't take me more than a moment before I responded confidently, "We do. I do."

Burke simply nodded in agreement and held me until my breathing calmed. He suggested that we turn to the scriptures for guidance and asked if I felt there was somewhere in particular that I would like to read. I shook my head and suggested we pick up where we had left off the night before Aiden passed. We had been studying the New Testament and had just finished the book of James. We turned next to 1 Peter 1 and had hardly begun when God answered our reaching.

To my dying day, this moment will stand out as one of the most powerful witnesses I have experienced that God truly speaks to us now, today, right to the core of our individual suffering through the words of His holy prophets. He answered our prayer moments after we pled for peace and understanding in a way that, years later, still pierces my soul with its truth and power.

As a background reference to the significance of what we read, the names of our twins are important to note. Aiden means "Little Fire," the perfect fit for our fighter who clung to life and whose persevering spirit amazed our doctors with his tenacity. And Alan, meaning "Little Rock," was the perfect complement to his brother, steady, strong and full of fortitude.

As we resumed reading in 1 Peter, the significance of Aiden's name choice jumped out at us. These words had been written thousands of years ago, yet undoubtedly, at that moment, they were meant just for us.

> Wherein ye greatly rejoice, though now for a season, if need be, ye are in heaviness through manifold temptations.
>
> That the trial of your faith, being much more precious than of gold that perisheth, though it be tried with *fire* might be found unto praise and honor and glory at the appearing of Jesus Christ:
>
> Whom having not seen, ye love; in whom, though now ye see him not, yet believing, ye rejoice with joy unspeakable and full of glory:
>
> Receiving the end of your faith, even the salvation of your soul. (1 Peter 1:6–9, emphasis added).

Burke and I could hardly believe what we had just read. Verse 6 spoke directly to our heaviness of heart, but mercifully reminded us that it would only be for a season. I especially liked the phrase "if need be," as if granting permission for us to grieve, not as a sign of weakness or doubt, but simply as a result of this mortal experience. Verse 7 assured us that this trial of our faith, tried "with fire" (our Little Fire), would end up being an experience that would be "more precious than gold" as it would ultimately bring honor and glory to Jesus Christ.

Although I know verse 8 refers directly to Jesus, we felt as though it was also referring to our baby boy, our Aiden, "whom having not seen, ye love." Words were never penned with more truth and power. They pierced my very soul. As verses 8 and 9 affirmed, though we could not see our baby, we rejoiced in the truths found in The Church of Jesus Christ of Latter-Day Saints, that families are forever, that through faith in Christ we can receive joy even while suffering and obtain the salvation of our souls.

Elder Jeffrey R. Holland echoed these thoughts: "You can have sacred, revelatory, profoundly instructive experiences with the Lord in any situation you are in. Indeed, you can have sacred, revelatory, profoundly instructive experiences with the Lord in the most miserable experiences of your life—in the worst settings, while enduring the most painful injustices, when facing the most insurmountable odds and opposition you have ever faced."[4]

This sacred experience reassured us that our Heavenly Father was completely aware and understanding of our heartache. After all, He knows exactly how it felt to lose a perfect son. Knowing that God knew our pain helped us to keep an eternal perspective. He had sent His Son to suffer the Atonement so He would know *exactly* how to succor us in our time of need. I love the words of Isaiah: "He hath borne our griefs, and carried our sorrows" and "was wounded for our transgressions, bruised for our iniquities" (Isaiah 53:4–5).

I found that many of the women I interviewed had also come to know Christ not despite their grief, but rather because of it.

Hannah

When Hannah's parents divorced, she was fifteen years old, supposedly the worst age for a girl to be to suffer such an experience. Although she would never say it out loud, she worried deep down that it was her fault. If only she had not given her mom such a hard time. If only she and her sisters had been kinder to each other. She filled her time with the drill team, boys, and being involved with everything the high school had to offer—busyness to mask brokenness. But just as she couldn't fix her parents' marriage, neither could she fix her broken heart on her own.

After years of trying to overcome this pain through her own will-power, Hannah finally had enough. "I had reached the end of my rope. I was totally done. I felt that I couldn't carry the weight for even one day longer. So, I just gave it to Him. As I prayed, I visualized packing all of my pain up in a box and literally handing it over to the Savior."

For some, this act of allowing Christ to take their suffering would not have worked. Miraculously for Hannah, it was just the gesture she needed to rid herself of the weights that had pulled her down. "I found complete peace in the Atonement of Christ. I don't know how to explain it or how it worked. All I know is that it did."

Camille

The bleating of two thousand sheep and the never-ending to-do list of the ranch called to her husband, Carter, Monday through Sunday, so Camille attended church alone. She was used to it after thirty years. She was a master at keeping everything afloat; her home, her business, her church callings, and the ranch where she kept everyone fed—fat and happy—during the chaos of lambing season.

But for the past few years, it felt like she was losing her grip, like she was slowly being unraveled from the inside out. How can you handle the terror in your heart when you open your son's bedroom door each morning and wonder if this will be the day that he won't wake up? The strain of his drug addiction stole her sleep and plagued her with stress headaches and ulcer-like worry in her stomach. Camille feared the pressure cooker within might finally explode. Her mother's prayer on behalf of her boy never ceased. *Please, Father, help him get clean. Please save him from himself. Please help me to know how to fix this.*

Of course, that was when the church calling had come. The bishop asked Camille to become the next Relief Society president of the ward in the middle of her family crisis. Her mother and daughter both counseled her not to accept.

"My daughter's my rock, my confidant. My *brain,* really. She told me, 'Mom, you already have way too much that you are dealing with.' I told the bishop he would have to talk to my husband, Carter, and make sure it was okay with him before I would consider it."

It took the bishop six weeks to make it down to the ranch. When he finally did, Carter surprised Camille by offering to support her in the calling. She was set apart in a sheep wagon at the ranch, which seemed only fitting, an indication of the hard work ahead of caring for Christ's lambs.

Sometimes when you're the Relief Society president, people assume you have it all together. Camille was a beloved president due to the perfect blend of her sunny personality, deep faith, and down-to-earth authenticity. She was quick to dispel the illusion that being in a presidency equaled perfection as she shared her heart with the sisters, laying bare the sorrows that persisted even when serving faithfully in a calling she never asked for.

"I think God was just waiting for me, waiting to see what I would say, and then when I said I would, He blessed me"—Camille's voice choked with emotion—"beyond measure."

This didn't mean that Camille's trials went away. Throughout the four years of her service as president, she struggled daily with the stress of her son's addiction, his subsequent arrests, and eventual rehabilitation process. Day by day, she focused on the Lord and constantly poured her heart out to him. In a way she had not thought possible, He alleviated her suffering. "Otherwise," she said, "I could not possibly have gotten through it."

Elizabeth

"I shouldn't be surprised." Elizabeth attempted a laugh while dabbing at her eyes with a tissue. "I mean, I gave my parents just as much grief, if not more, when I was her age. I should probably just be grateful it hasn't escalated to that level."

Elizabeth had been facing significant challenges in her marriage for several years, but now that she and her husband of more than twenty years were officially divorcing, her entire world was crumbling around her. Everything was a mess. She was experiencing feelings of deep sadness and powerlessness. The children were hurting, most especially her teenage daughter who was self-detonating, systematically destroying anything good in her life in response to the anguish eating her up inside.

"I mean, what do you do for your child when you feel like it's your fault that she's hurting in the first place?"

Elizabeth battled within herself, trying to strike a balance of taking responsibility for the natural consequences of her actions, while simultaneously appealing to God for His help. She had never understood until now what people meant when they talked about fully relying on the Lord.

"I am doing more than I've ever done before in trying to live the gospel. I am on my knees constantly. I seek guidance through scripture study and priesthood blessings. The temple has become my sanctuary and I go as often as I can. I see now, more than ever before, the only way I am going to make it through all of this is by relying on His grace to carry me. His tender mercies are real and ever present, even amidst the storms. I have grown closer to my Heavenly Father and feel a deep love for my Savior Jesus Christ. That alone has become a huge blessing in my life. I've also learned that I need to trust that His grace is sufficient for my daughter as well. He knows and loves her even more than I do. He will be there for both of us."

Sara

Sara is a great lover of music. When she couldn't find the words to describe how she was feeling, she pulled out her phone and played a song called "Quiet Uptown" from the musical *Hamilton*. We listened to the beautiful song, tears gathering in our eyes.

> There are moments that the words don't reach
> There is suffering too terrible to name
> You hold your child as tight as you can
> And push away the unimaginable
> The moments when you're in so deep
> It feels easier to just swim down.[5]

Sara pauses the song. "When your husband has struggled with pornography for years, and years, and years, you reach a point where it's all too much. It's like you can't allow yourself to care anymore because your heart has been ripped out so many times. All you can do is just swim down."

She presses play, and we continue to listen. The music tells the story of another family's heartache, but sitting in my living room, discussing this all-consuming sorrow, it feels as if it was written just for Sara.

> There are moments that the words don't reach
> There is grace too powerful to name
> We push away what we can never understand
> We push away the unimaginable
> They are standing in the garden
> Alexander by Eliza's side
> She takes his hand.[6]

Sara stops the song again. "And yet . . ." Here the tears she has been holding back begin to flow in earnest. "I know how very flawed I am as well. I know God has had to forgive me for the same mistakes over and over again. And ultimately . . . I love him. So we keep trying, as imperfect as we are."

It's silent for just a moment as we let that truth sink in. Her finger lightly taps the play button.

> Forgiveness. Can you imagine?
> Forgiveness. Can you imagine?
> If you see him in the street
> Walking by her side,
> Talking by her side, have pity
> They are going through the unimaginable.[7]

*　*　*

Peace is not the absence of trouble. It is the presence of Christ in the midst of trouble. The Savior said, "Peace I leave with you; my peace I give you. Not as the world gives do I give to you. Let not your hearts be troubled, neither let them be afraid" (John 14:27).

Sometimes in the thick of our sorrow, peace may seem completely unobtainable. We may feel that our endeavors to swim forward are wasted as the finish line seems to grow farther and farther away the more we try. We may feel that our efforts are never enough. And the truth is, they're not. None of us are capable of conquering the pain of our suffering on our own. None of us can heal properly just by "trying harder."

Sometimes, we are tested above and beyond our breaking point with one challenge following on the heels of another. Many times, we may feel like we are drowning, and the moment our heads break above water, gasping for breath, another wave comes crashing down. If we have any hope of surviving the tempest, we must grab hold of the preserver, the life line that is our Savior. As the inspiring women on Multiply Goodness (an online interfaith community that studies the Bible together) shared, "It's the companionship of the Lord that brings us hope in times when life is too difficult to bear, when we've been treading water for so long, our legs are finally starting to give out. It's His strength that not only brings us to the surface, but lifts us right out of the water and places us on a rock.[8]

ENDNOTES

1. Robert D. Hales, "Your Sorrow Shall Be Turned to Joy," 1983
2. Jean B. Bingham, "That Your Joy Might Be Full," churchofjesuschrist.org/study/general-conference/2017/10/that-your-joy-might-be-full?lang=eng, October 2017.
3. Dale G. Renlund, "Consider the Goodness and Greatness of God," churchofjesuschrist.org/study/general-conference/2020/04/26renlund?lang=eng, April 2020.
4. Jeffrey R. Holland, "Lessons from Liberty Jail," speeches.byu.edu/talks/jeffrey-r-holland/lessons-liberty-jail/ 2008.
5. Lin-Manuel Miranda and original Broadway cast. *Hamilton: An American Musical*. Atlantic Records, 2015.
6. Ibid.
7. Ibid.
8. Multiply Goodness Facebook post, facebook.com/multiplygoodness, May 29, 2019.

CHAPTER 10

See That You Are Merciful

*"See that you are merciful unto your brethren,
deal justly, judge righteously, and do
good continually."*

—Alma 41:14

There once was a group of neighbors who had come together for a special occasion. As they entered the building, each guest carried a heavy sack upon their back. With a sign from the host, the company opened their sacks and dumped the contents on the table. Out tumbled the secret struggles of each person present; the problems and the heartaches lying undisguised in a tangled heap of troubles for all to view.

You see, all present had agreed to this opportunity to evaluate the contents of their neighbors' bags in hopes to exchange a lighter load for their own. But to their dismay, the guests were so shocked by the cargo in the other bags, no one's load seemed more appealing than their own worn out issues. After surveying the heavy hardships on the table, each person opened their sack, quietly scooped in their formerly disdainful troubles, and hefted the familiar burden onto their backs once more, grateful to be carrying their load and not another's.

We don't necessarily need to know the details of what others are going through to choose to be compassionate. Neal A. Maxwell said,

"Extending our mercy to someone need not wait upon our full understanding of their challenges."[1]

When my in-laws were called to serve as ordinance workers in the temple, they were trained to treat each person who entered the House of the Lord with love, respect, and kindness. In a training video for temple workers, Elder Henry B. Eyring shared, "Many years ago, I was first counselor to a district president in the eastern United States. More than once, as we were driving to our little branches, he said to me, 'Hal, when you meet someone, treat them as if they were in serious trouble, and you will be right more than half the time.' Not only was he right, but I have learned over the years that he was too low in his estimate."[2]

Ordinance workers are taught to view each patron in attendance as though they had entered the temple that day seeking relief while wrestling with the greatest challenge of their life. This is key to making the temple a safe place and in creating an uplifting environment for all present.

I remembered my in-laws' training as I entered the temple for my first endowment session following Aiden's death. It had been only a few short months since his passing, and my emotions were still very close to the surface. Near the end of the endowment ceremony, I found myself weeping with temple workers all around who seemed to be at a loss as to what to do or say. I felt embarrassed by my outburst, but the sister assisting me with the final portion of the ceremony was so kind, simply patting my back and squeezing my shoulder repeatedly. Though she was a stranger, she helped me feel loved instead of judged.

We might know logically that life is not easy for any of us, yet our instinctual reaction is to make judgments of others. This is a biological, subconscious human trait. Judgments are a necessary part of ensuring our safety and survival. We make dozens of calculating perceptions in a fraction of a second without even being aware that we are doing it.

On The Church of Jesus Christ of Latter-Day Saints' website, there is a section under gospel topics that addresses "Judging Others." In part, it explains, "Our righteous judgments about others can provide needed guidance for them and, in some cases, protection for us and our families. We should approach any such judgment with care and compassion. As much as we can, we should judge people's situations rather than judging the people themselves. Whenever possible, we should refrain from making judgments until we have an adequate knowledge of the facts. And we should always be sensitive to the Holy Spirit, who can guide our decisions."[3]

When we encounter an unfamiliar situation, our perceptive brain instantly goes to work gathering intel about the environment and people we meet. This is natural and necessary to make sense of the world and our place in it. However, it is important that we become aware of the information our brain is offering us through our thoughts so we can make a conscious choice how we will view the world and the people in it.

For example, think about moving to a new home and attending church at a new ward. As soon as we enter the parking lot, we begin to take notes and start creating opinions. We size up the neighborhood, the building, and the cars. As we walk inside, we observe the smells, the state of the carpet, and the noise level. We make assumptions about the people in attendance based on the way they talk, look, and behave. Depending on our level of self-awareness, we notice *them* noticing *us,* and begin to form conclusions as to how well we have been accepted in a matter of seconds.

If we make our judgments in such a short time, it's clear that we could easily *mis*judge. As Jody Moore teaches, instead of accepting the information our well-meaning brain offers us as certain, it would serve us better to be willing to question the thoughts that pop into our brain as optional opinions, rather than fact. Returning to our new ward scenario, rather than assuming everyone is making positive or negative judgments of us (or us judging them), perhaps we can give them the benefit of the doubt, and ourselves the benefit of more time, to discover the reality of our situation. One popular saying that has served me well over the years is be kind, for everyone you meet is fighting a hard battle.

When I began this project, I thought I had a basic understanding of the battles the women of my ward had faced. Initially, I thought I would interview a handful of women and write a chapter for each one sharing their story. However, as I visited these women, what I had naively assumed would be an hour-long discussion began to turn into two, three, four and, one time, even a five-hour long dialogue. I quickly realized that a chapter would never be sufficient. I could write an entire book on each person.

I explored the idea of separating each lady into a category like a filing system. All who had suffered from infertility compartmentalized nicely into one chapter. Those affected with mental illness snuggled cozily between chapters on addiction and suicide. Clearly, that formula wouldn't work either. How could I confine a woman's life experience to one tragic topic? On top of that, through our interviews, I was humbled to learn that my knowledge of each woman was always lacking and what I had perceived as her one big trial in life was often misplaced. One of my first interviewees is the perfect case in point.

I came into our discussion assuming that the most pressing trial of her life had been her health challenges. However, she completely shattered all my preconceived notions when she said, "I got hung up on the word *sorrow* because I didn't feel like I had experienced anything truly sorrowful in my life. But when I looked up the definition, it said that the synonyms are grief, deep disappointment, and suffering. I realized that the thing that brings me the greatest sense of these feelings in my life is definitely my husband's pornography addiction."

I had been friends with this woman for several years, and I hadn't had a clue. Suddenly the purpose of my project evolved. Not only did I want to acknowledge the difficulties these women had faced, but plead for less judgment among us. We truly never know what the people around us have experienced in their lives.

Early on, I created a spreadsheet to keep track of basic interview information. One of my column headers read, "Things I Think We Will Discuss," which I filled out prior to the interview. The following column read, "Things We Actually Discussed." As you can probably guess, every interview revealed unimagined insights into each woman's life, unveiling issues and insecurities along with talents, tenacity, and testimonies that I would have never guessed they had within them.

Why is this? What is it about society that makes us so quick to hide our hurts, sometimes and most especially from the people who know and love us best? Why, when we are asked how we are doing, do we reply with the obligatory, "I'm fine," when we are anything *but* fine? Why do we grow so uncomfortable when others admit to weakness or pain, especially online?

You've seen it, haven't you? It feels as though the moment a social media status portrays anything less than a humble-brag, a travelogue, or a funny meme, there is a tendency to grow uncomfortable, to ignore the vulnerable in search of endless entertainment. So, we scroll on. We disconnect. We bury our stories in order to protect our hearts.

Yet, this is the antithesis to fostering healing and growth. I have found that if this same admission to vulnerability were given in person, rather than online, the result would be one of deep human connection rather than casting our metaphorical emotional pearls before social media swine.

Sharing our stories has been lauded again and again as one of the most powerful remedies to pain. Brené Brown, the esteemed research professor and expert on vulnerability, shame, and empathy, said, "No one wants to talk about shame, pain, and fear, and the less we talk about it the more we have it."[4]

Time and time again, my interviewees said, "I've never talked with anyone about this before." Or, as another woman exclaimed, "This is like the best free therapy I've ever had!" They came weighed down with burdens and left our conversation so much lighter, because of their willingness to communicate and connect. They often expressed, "It feels so liberating to actually talk about this."

For some, our suffering may be played out on a more visible stage than others through public adversity such as the death of a loved one, a messy divorce, or a debilitating accident. But often, the raw pain from more private trials is tucked away into secure corners of our hearts. Although many tend to hide their sorrows, only moved upon to share on rare occasions, others choose a more open approach, baring their heart frequently. Neither approach is better than the other. Each individual has the freedom to choose how their sorrow will play out in relation to others.

A simple question to ask ourselves to determine whether it is appropriate to share our private stories and feelings is, "Will anyone benefit from sharing this information?" In a conversation with my father and psychologist Dr. David Bush, we explored the concept further. He said, "Too often we stonewall to protect ourselves or else we verbally vomit all over others who are not prepared for the emotional intensity of our revelations. Finding a balance takes experience. Sometimes we fail to share when we feel impressed to disclose, and other times we share excessively and afterward we wish we had been more cautious, especially if the disclosure costs us dearly. It is wise to practice sharing a little with someone we know we can trust and who will give us honest feedback. As we learn to discriminate promptings to share from mere emotion or false sense of obligation, we allow ourselves to be appropriately vulnerable and share in ways that benefit ourselves and others."[5]

Being vulnerable is essentially showing up without armor. If we choose to share our stories, we must prepare ourselves for possibly painful consequences. We cannot control the responses of other human beings and, unfortunately, not everyone will respond in a lovely way. On the one hand, we stand to gain deeper connections, healing from communicating, and perhaps giving our listener(s) the gift of greater understanding. On the other hand, we may incur more harm at the hands of someone's thoughtless or unkind words.

You may have noticed a variety of responses when the subject of your grief surfaces. Some people change the subject, others may turn to humor to try and diffuse their discomfort, and still others may flounder about throwing out trite clichés such as, "You're stronger than you know," to comfort us or simply to fill the silence.

All too often people say the "wrong thing" in an awkward attempt to say something profound or helpful. Just as we would hope that others will not judge us because of our struggles, it is important to give people the same compassion and grace in return, even if their attempts to be kind end up creating unintentional wounds.

For example, my husband's cousin lost the love of her life after only a few short years of marriage. One man who spoke with her at her husband's funeral caused unforeseen hurt by declaring, "I know *exactly* how you feel. I just went through an awful divorce." For this young widow in deep mourning, the man's attempt to sympathize was incredibly offensive. However, she taught me a profound lesson when she later acknowledged, "I'm sure for him, that divorce was the most painful thing he had gone through. Although it was a terrible thing to say, he was just trying to relate to me and show me that, he too, knew how it felt to be sad about something."

Although resisting the urge to judge should go both ways, there are some phrases you may want to avoid when conversing with someone who is still in a state of sadness over their trial. Sometimes what one person may view as helpful feedback can be extremely hurtful for another. The experience of no two people is exactly alike. For that reason, it's usually a mistake to say, "I know how you feel." Even if your scenarios are similar, this comment can cause many people to bristle and become defensive. A few other statements to avoid are, "You shouldn't feel that way," or "Maybe it's time to let it go." Whether well intended or not, we should never presume to tell another person how they *should* feel or impose a timeline upon another's grief.

Quite possibly the most painful statement I heard over and over again after our loss was the dreaded words, *at least*. *At least* your baby died before you could make memories with him since that would be so much harder to deal with. *At least* you still have your other children. *At least* you knew he was struggling so his death didn't come as a surprise. *At least* he wasn't a toddler who got hit by a car like my nephew. *At least* you got to carry him almost full term before he died. Any time you may think to use the phrase *at least* to help someone else, please think again.

When in doubt, the most powerful words you can say to someone who is sorrowing are, "I'm sorry. I love you. What can I do for you?" Though these may seem too obvious or plain, there is purity in simplicity.

Most of the time, people don't need you to solve their problems. They don't need to hear how your sister's coworker's aunt also had a stillborn, or had a son commit suicide, or was diagnosed with cancer. If you are going to visit someone who has had something painful happen recently, please go to listen, not to share anecdotes of similar situations or to process your own emotional baggage. Often the recently bereaved are barely surviving their own pain and cannot handle the stories of others who are also hurting. When someone is freshly in Victimhood, it is nearly impossible to process other people's emotions in addition to your own.

Nevertheless, sometimes as Survivors, others going through similar pain may seek us out. Our past experiences from our trials can help us counsel people looking for guidance. Even if we've no advice to give, simply knowing that someone cares and understands is enough to bring comfort and strength. Sheryl Sandberg wisely stated, "Real empathy is sometimes not insisting that it will be okay, but acknowledging that it is not."[6]

Rather than defaulting to judgment when we notice someone is not okay, our time as suffering Victims should lend greater compassion to the way we think, speak, and act toward others. As a Survivor, we have gained the ability to look back and remember the pain we once experienced so we can relate to others through increased empathy. Even if another person's trial is vastly different from our own, we can draw on our common feelings of grief over our challenges and try to put ourselves in the other person's shoes.

When I interviewed Tessa, I was impressed by her ability to addresses the struggles of her life matter-of-factly, yet with compassion toward who she was as well as the other players in her story. She did not try to rewrite history by pretending she was okay with everything that had happened to her, but she was still able to objectively view the lessons she gained and the people who helped her through.

Tessa

The first time I met Tessa, she was warm and friendly with zero pretense and an overall aura of genuine affability. I liked her immediately, and we soon invited her family to dinner to get to know them better.

When the night of the dinner arrived, I opened the door to welcome her family. Tessa sported a summer tank top. As she entered our home carrying a delicious dessert tray, I noticed numerous scars marring both her arms from shoulder to elbow. My mind instantly flashed back to a loved one's compulsion to cutting as a teen. I immediately deduced that each crisscrossed line was due to self-harming. Tessa was obviously comfortable in her damaged skin, and I grew curious, wondering how she came to wear her scars without shame instead of hiding them behind long-sleeved shirts, afraid of discovery.

Over three years later, I finally had the chance to ask. Knowing that Tessa had an awful first marriage resulting in divorce, I assumed her sorrows were centered around that relationship, the hardships of being a single mother, and perhaps the origins behind her scars.

When I asked Tessa what she would identify as sorrows in her life, she brought a deepening context to her story. "My biggest trials almost all started when I was young, with my parents' deaths. I don't think I would have ever married my first husband if I hadn't been so traumatized from those experiences."

In a period of less than two years, Tessa found herself the head of her household at age sixteen, after her father passed from cancer and her mother suffered a heart attack, likely a result of years of drug abuse. "I remember trying to go to bed the night my mom died. I remember laying there and thinking, 'What do we do now? What happens when your parents both die?'"

Although emotionally frail and perhaps ill-prepared to be on her own, Tessa moved away not long after to attend university. "I didn't feel like I had any other option. When my dad died and my mom couldn't get a job with a high school education, she told me over and over again, 'You have to get a college education—you have to be able to take care of your family because you don't know what will happen.' That had a huge effect on me."

Her first year of college was a struggle, but overall, Tessa felt things were going okay until her high school boyfriend broke up with her. She felt as though she was losing the last stable person in her support network. Mentally and emotionally, she couldn't handle another heartbreak.

In desperation, Tessa began to self-harm in order to feel some sense of control over her life. "I needed *something*. I needed something that I could control. Something that would take my focus off of my emotions, because I didn't know how to handle them. And, you know, it was addicting. It was something that I was in charge of, even though I wasn't really, that was the mentality. It's not a healthy way to cope, but it was a way."

Cutting became a frequent out for Tessa. Whenever she felt overwhelmed or depressed, she would lock herself in her room and self-harm. Her roommates confided years later that they were afraid when she closed the door. They knew what she was doing, but they had no idea how to help her. They attended a student ward together each Sunday, but church began to feel oppressive to Tessa as she sat in the pew experiencing intense guilt and shame for harming herself. Unaware that others had faced such a challenge, she felt completely alone and disgusted by her inability to stop cutting. She wondered, "Why can't I stop damaging my body?"

Tessa's bishop at the time became a source of support to her at this challenging period. She recalled, "My bishop owned a business in town, and sometimes when I had been cutting, I would show up at his work for help. He would take one look at me, help me to a bathroom, get paper towels and just clean me up. And that meant a lot because I felt so ashamed of myself, you know? But he wasn't afraid of it, and he didn't say, 'What are you doing to yourself?' He would just say, always so kindly, 'Let's get you cleaned up.' And that's all he did. And it meant so much."

To Tessa, her bishop's behavior was true love in action. He never expressed condemnation or judgment. Tessa marked his genuine kindness and acceptance as the beginning of her road toward recovery.

Janie

Often, we think of the term "judging" as a negative connotation only, but sometimes people pass positive judgments of others as well. We may hear statements such as, "They are such a great family," while behind closed doors sadness reigns.

Janie grew up in an active LDS family, but the lip service given at church did not translate into a Christ-like home. She shared, "The greatest sorrow of my life comes from not being born of goodly parents." It was upsetting to Janie, watching her step-dad attempt to create the illusion of being a good man in public, while at home he was cruel, demeaning, and emotionally abusive.

With unhealthy examples at home, Janie searched for a genuine family she could emulate. As a teenager, she was influenced by the good example of her boyfriend and his faithful family. "I remember thinking, this is what a real family looks like. I was determined to have a family like that someday. I prayed, and I worked my butt off to get out of the toxic environment I was in. When I met Isaac, it was kind of like this feeling that I had finally found home, you know? I knew that we could create what I had always wanted; a home that was loving both in public and in private."

Knowing that not every kid is growing up in an "ideal" environment and recognizing that many adults still suffer from the dysfunction of their childhood should lend to greater compassion as we interact with others. Janie is a great illustration of rising above adversity and making what you want out of life.

"I'm proud of the life we have created. We have had to work so hard for it, but we can see the fruit of our labor in our four girls and home. It is so, so sweet to finally be on this end."

Mitchell and Rebecca

Rebecca was a newly divorced single mother of three when she and Mitchell became friends. After the betrayal of a nine-year marriage gone awry, she was determined she would never marry again and refused to get to know any men who would pose a threat to her resolve. However, as a man with same gender attraction (SGA), Mitchell didn't count. He was safe.

The friendship blossomed as Rebecca tutored Mitchell in math and he, in turn, took an interest in her three small children. With no fear of a romantic relationship developing, the two let down their guards and became increasingly comfortable with one another, sharing their thoughts and experiences openly, grateful to have a safe person to confide in.

Mitchell knew from the time he was a small child that he was "different" from the other boys in his neighborhood. Though he was raised in a loving, faithful home, for much of his life he fought against what felt like a brokenness inside of him. So many had the opinion that simply being attracted to the same-sex was a sin, even though the Apostles clearly taught that the attraction alone is not wrong, rather the acting-out on those feelings.

Mitchell said, "The thing about same gender attraction is that it has become essentially the spiritual leprosy of today. People see it and they misunderstand it, and because of that misunderstanding, they shun it." After years of repressing his tendencies in order to fit in, Mitchell decided to embrace a homosexual identity for a season as he sought for clarity, while still attempting to remain faithful to his religious upbringing. During this experimental time, he found it nearly impossible to maintain the testimony of his youth and wavered in a fragile state of confusion and sorrow.

In his quest for answers, Mitchell discovered a verse of scripture that touched him deeply. It read, "Therefore, he giveth this promise unto you, with an immutable covenant that they shall be fulfilled; and all things wherewith you have been afflicted shall work together for your good, and to my name's glory, saith the Lord" (D&C 98:3). Was it possible that Mitchell's SGA could be used for his good and to glorify God?

Missing the solid ground of the gospel, he chose to return to The Church of Jesus Christ of Latter-Day Saints, resolved to deal with his feelings of attraction and commit to a life dedicated to Christ. As much as he longed for love and a family of his own, he believed that these blessings would be forever out of his reach. However, he felt strongly that any sacrifice required of him was worth the effort in order to follow Heavenly Father's plan.

One Sunday, not long after Mitchell's special friendship with Rebecca and her children began, he was attending a singles ward where the elders quorum met in the same room intended for the Primary children of other wards who met in the building. As he sat down for the lesson, his eyes fell upon a sign that read, "Heavenly Father Prepared You to Come to a Family." The Spirit overwhelmed him as his thoughts instantly went to Rebecca. He explained, "Now, I knew that bulletin had been placed there for the Primary children, but at that time it spoke directly to me. God had been preparing me to come to this family."

In a series of personal revelation designed specifically for Mitchell and Rebecca, the two agreed that they were supposed to marry, uniting with eyes wide open in an inter-orientation marriage. Rebecca said, "We knew what we were getting into. We knew that it was going to be tough with the divorce and having a blended family. We knew that people were not going to understand our relationship. God knowing that [it was right for us] is what I go back to."

Although their families were wonderful and supportive, many others have questioned their decision and passed judgments. As they reflected on the twelve years of their relationship, the two agreed that none of the sorrow connected with Mitchell's same gender attraction was due to problems in their relationship. Rebecca explained further, "There has been sorrow, but it was all due to external things that we have had to deal with because of it. The *stigma* has caused sorrow, but not between us. In fact, I think it has caused a strength and a level of emotional and spiritual intimacy."

Although their marriage and family has been filled with great unity and love, the Johnsons have suffered from the ignorance and unkindness of others. They shared, "For us, as a family and as a couple, it has been very isolating. We should remember how Jesus treated the lepers. He could have become diseased by associating with them, but He chose instead to show others that they were still beloved of God. That's what we need to do. We need to get away from speaking in 'they's' and talking in generalities. We need to look beyond, get to know people individually, and say, 'This is a person. This is a family unit. This is a couple. They have kids.' There is so much sorrow in stigma. We have to get past that and get to know the person behind it."

The Johnsons are working hard to steer clear of the dirty pain that comes from being misjudged and looking for the lessons they can take from the poor treatment they have received at the hands of others. Mitchell shared, "One of my favorite quotes comes from Martin Luther King Jr., who said, 'Unearned suffering is redemptive.' I just love that, because through the Savior, unearned suffering *is* redemptive. If you are tolerant and you are long suffering, you may make a friend out of all the people who you thought were your enemy. That's why I feel there is a tangible power to loving your enemy. You can see that person in a whole new light. I believe the adversary has put these walls between us, but once I was willing to be tolerant with intolerance, I found that we can learn from other people who come from a vastly different mindset than our own. It's a careful dance of learning to understand one another."

Laynah

Laynah's journey with infertility was made especially difficult by the judgments expressed by acquaintances who made thoughtless remarks. "People would say things like, 'Isn't it time you got started on a family?' And I would just be so crushed. We were going through these intense fertility treatments, so my emotions were just all over the place anyway, but it just felt so awful to have people make these comments when they didn't know how badly I wanted to be a mother."

As painful as those years were for Laynah, she was grateful for the skill it had honed in her to be able to identify people who were hurting and knowing what *not* to say.

* * *

Perhaps the most precious gem dug from the mountain of adversity is empathy. As Survivors, it is essential that we are able to examine that jewel of understanding and use it to bless the lives of others. Whether you now obtain a database in your head of what to say or what not to say when others are hurting, or if you are moved upon to help others who are currently enduring a similar trial, these are signposts that you are officially growing, healing, and moving forward. The more we turn outward, the more success we have in transforming into a Contributor, the final stage of our Growth Through Grief.

ENDNOTES

1. Neal A. Maxwell, "Remember How Merciful the Lord Hath Been," churchofjesuschrist.org/study/general-conference/2004/04/remember-how-merciful-the-lord-hath-been?lang=eng, April 2004.
2. Henry B. Eyring, "Try, Try, Try," churchofjesuschrist.org/study/general-conference/2018/10/try-try-try?lang=eng Henry B. Eyring, October 2018.
3. "Judging Others," churchofjesuschrist.org/study/manual/gospel-topics/judging-others?lang=eng
4. Brené Brown, "The Power of Vulnerability," TEDxHouston, June 2010, ted.com/talks/brene_brown_the_power_of_vulnerability?language=en.
5. David Bush, email to Emily Adams, May 8, 2020.
6. Sheryl Sandberg, Facebook post, June 3, 2015.

CHAPTER 11

Now Me

Phase 3: Contributor

*"I say unto you, that ye shall weep and lament, but
the world shall rejoice: and ye shall be sorrowful,
but your sorrow shall be turned into joy."*

—John 16:16

In the midst of his battle with cancer, Elder Neal A. Maxwell shared this valuable insight, "I was doing some pensive pondering and these thirteen instructive and reassuring words came into my mind: *I have given you Leukemia that you might teach my people with authenticity.*"[1]

A synonym for the word *authentic* is *genuine*. Essentially, Elder Maxwell was taught that in order for him to teach God's children with power, he had to be able relate to people. In order to genuinely, authentically connect, he had to understand misery on a level that would knit his heart together with others who were struggling with their own afflictions. Seeing their individual pain reflected in the challenges faced by the Lord's living Apostle opened hearts to his message that may have been formerly closed.

Although Elder Maxwell endured horrendous agony from the cancer that eventually took his life, he was given a gift to know that there was a reason for his suffering. Being a victim of cancer would change his ability to minister to God's children in a way that he was formerly unable to achieve. Like Elder Maxwell, a hallmark of those Survivors who are ready to mature to Contributors are those who have discovered a purpose for their pain. These individuals have developed strength over the course of the first two phases of their Growth Through Grief journeys. As Victims and then Survivors, they have observed the way their trial has changed them, the lessons they have learned, and are now motivated to turn outward. Many have a strong desire to transform their suffering into a tool, utilizing their sorrow to make the world a better place.

Utility in sorrow. Purpose in pain. Some may ask, is that even possible? I would argue that the most important lesson this project has taught me is that we *can* find purpose in the pain of our lives. And, as audacious as it sounds, we can even find beauty.

When I heard of the bitter fruits of adversity the women I interviewed had swallowed, and then saw the remarkably sweet fruits born from their sorrows, I saw suffering through an advanced lens. Because of the way many of these women chose to respond to their trials, they have created a beauty that is inspiring and life changing to behold. With new eyes, we can see life, grief, and others in a fresh light and we are motivated to become other-focused, rather than self-absorbed in our pain.

The loss of our son irrevocably changed me for the better by endowing me with the ability to see the heartache in others and developing an earnest desire to lift where I stand. Likewise, because of their sorrow, these women have been gifted the ability to not only notice suffering in others, but more important, they feel motivated to alleviate their heavy loads. Indeed, they have learned how to more fully honor their covenant to "bear one another's burdens, that they may be light; yea, . . . mourn with those that mourn; and comfort those that stand in need of comfort" (Mosiah 18:18–9).

These are the golden threads of wisdom hidden within the messy haystack of our afflictions. Once found, it is critical for us to share these priceless treasures so the wealthy fruits of the Spirit may enrich all of our Heavenly Father's children.

In the Book of Mormon, the Nephite sons of King Mosiah are examples of those who were changed by the sweetness of the fruit and were relentless in their efforts to share that joy with others. Initially, these young men are introduced as rebellious children of a faithful father. These wayward boys eventually repent, deny their rights to the throne, and instead choose a life of humble servitude to God. They feel compelled to proclaim the goodness of God and the invaluable lessons they have learned with any who will hear them. Leaving their life of privilege, they strike out on what would become a fourteen-year mission to the Lamanites, a wild and ferocious people who delighted in murdering the Nephites. They must have been full of trepidation about their journey, uncertain if any would listen or if they might even lose their lives as martyrs in the Lord's cause. Knowing their unease, the Lord comforts his sons, breathing courage into convictions with His message: "And the Lord said unto them also: Go forth among the Lamanites, thy brethren, and establish my word; yet ye shall be patient in longsuffering and afflictions, that ye may show forth good examples unto them in me, and I will make an instrument of thee in my hands unto the salvation of many souls" (Alma 17:11).

Becoming a tool in the hand of God to be wielded for good is the preeminent prize for Growth Through Grief. Though there are myriad reasons we suffer, we can choose to believe we have been assigned our mountain to show others it can be moved. We can feel a sense of triumph and assess the burden that once felt so heavy upon our shoulders and realize how strong we have become *because* of the weight. Rather than being perpetually stuck in Victimhood asking, "Why me?", we can stand with a sense of confident responsibility declaring instead, "Now me," ready to reach out a hand to those who have come after us.

Overcoming adversity empowers us to lift one another, to grow together, and to experience joy with one another. In a poem attributed to the ancient Persian poet, Rumi, he beautifully describes, "Sorrow prepares you for joy. It violently sweeps everything out of your house, so that new joy can find space to enter. It shakes the yellow leaves from the bough of your heart, so that fresh, green leaves can grow in their place. It pulls up the rotten roots, so that new roots hidden beneath have room to grow. Whatever sorrow shakes from your heart, far better things will take their place."[2]

Linda

One woman who demonstrates the power of sorrow turned to joy through contribution is Linda. In her childhood she experienced sexual, physical, and emotional abuse. Although her parents were aware of the abuse, they did nothing to protect her from it. Linda rightly grieved the trauma of her childhood, but she refused to spend her life justifiably bitter in her Victimhood. Using her wisdom as a survivor, Linda turned her pain to contribution as she volunteered for fifteen years as a CASA, advocating for children in the foster care system.

CASA volunteers are court appointed special advocates assigned to sit in on all meetings with social workers, foster care families and coordinators, police, therapist, and so on, and ultimately testify in court as an unbiased voice interested solely in what is best for the abused child. Linda said, "I never had someone advocating *for me*, so I wanted to ensure that as many children as possible would have an advocate *because* of me." Knowing that she could assist helpless children gave purpose to the pain of Linda's past.

Riley

Riley is another wonderful example. At just seventeen she was diagnosed with severe rheumatoid arthritis and assumed she would be wheelchair bound by age thirty. Over time, she found her anger and grief for the life she would never have lessening, and instead a desire to contribute in meaningful ways formed. She started a blog and wrote about her experience with chronic illness to educate others and foster empathy. Despite the pain in her stiff joints, she started a business where she labored to create beautiful jewelry to bring awareness to causes such as cancer, autism, and arthritis.

Lacie

After the tragic loss of two premature babies, Lacie was appalled by the lack of support at the hospital or in the community for bereaved mothers. Despite her intense grief, she formed a chapter of Share—a bereavement group that has given support and services to numerous families.

Annie

Annie underwent the agony of giving a baby up for adoption at age fifteen. Rather than being ashamed of this experience, she has used her hard-won wisdom to speak to teenagers on the importance of their life choices and the benefits of adoption.

* * *

For me, remaining in the weeds in a state of agony over losing Aiden wasn't an option. What would be the purpose of losing him if his short life left only a legacy of heartbreak? With a deep and abiding faith that we will be reunited with our son after this life, our family has chosen to find purpose in our pain by turning the love meant for him outward and upward in our efforts to leave this world better than we found it.

In many ways, my path to becoming a Contributor has been inseparably connected with learning how to be vulnerable and brave. When I first became pregnant with the twins, I learned of a popular Facebook group for Latter-Day Saint women called "Mormon Moms of Multiples—MmoMs" (later changed to "Ministering Moms of Multiples" when President Nelson encouraged Church members to embrace the full name of the Church). This quickly became my favorite social media space as the thousands of members managed to be cordial and kind to one another, often asking for parenting advice or posting humorous updates on their twins, triplets, and even quadruplets. I felt it was a space where I "belonged" with faithful Christian women who loved the gospel and their families. However, once we learned Aiden had passed away, I suddenly felt like an imposter in the group. I wasn't technically a twin mom anymore, though in my heart I still labeled myself as one, and I worried that I may no longer be welcome among the MMoMs.

About six months after our loss, I began the therapeutic process of blogging about our journey with the twins. At that point I had kept a blog for nearly seven years, primarily as a way to journal and keep my family updated on our lives. One night after the cathartic experience of documenting the details of our story, I had an undeniable prompting to share the link to my blog on the MMoMs Facebook page. At first, I resisted the feeling, scared to put such tender and private experiences out for strangers to read and perhaps criticize. However, when the feeling wouldn't go away, I dug deep to muster up my courage and posted the link, praying that it would be well received. I had been unapologetically raw and unfiltered in my blogs, and I felt completely naked with vulnerability.

I never could have anticipated the outpouring of love that single leap of faith brought into my life. Complete strangers reached out to me with compassion and empathy, enfolding me into their midst with comments such as, "You will *always* be a mother of twins." And, "Your story has changed me forever. #aimforaiden." Another woman said, "My twins nearly made me lose my mind today. After sobbing through your blog, I snuck into their bedroom just to stare at their sleeping faces and remind myself how blessed I am to have them both here. Thank you for giving me the gift of gratitude for my children. I am so very sorry for your loss."

That single post led to relationships with other mothers who had lost one or more of their multiples and was the catalyst for me to form "Ministering Moms of Missing Multiples," an offshoot of MMoMs for bereaved women who could relate to the devastation of losing one twin while simultaneously rejoicing over the survival of the other. Though our scenarios are different, our similar pain has created a safe space for us to bond and offer support to one another as we continue to work through our grief.

Contribution may elicit a call to action in your life as it has for me, but it may also manifest itself in quieter ways. My sister-in-law, Catherine, has contributed greatly to my healing with nothing more than a phone call. About once every six months, she rings and says, "I just called because I wondered if you would like to talk about Aiden today." I've been given many thoughtful gifts in my life, but each time she does this, I am given the most priceless gift imaginable.

Elizabeth Edwards said, "If you know someone who has lost [someone], and you're afraid to mention them because you think you might make them sad by reminding them that they died—you're not reminding them. They didn't forget they died. What you're reminding them of is that you remembered that they lived."[2]

Catherine's invitation to talk about my son may not be notable to the world, but for me, it is a tremendous contribution to my healing. Often, those who have suffered loss fear that their loved ones will be forgotten. Many long to talk about them and have little opportunity or excuse to do so. Opening up a conversation in this way meets that deep-seated need to carry on their memory, to process sorrow, and to create deeply connected relationships.

In nature, these deep connections can be seen in emotionally advanced species such as elephants. Elephants are known for their fierce loyalty and the close bond of their matriarchal families. They move together in groups and have often been seen helping each other.

Andrea Crosta, Director of the Elephant Action League said, "When a member of an elephant herd dies, the other elephants gather around and gently touch the body with their trunks and feet. They press together and console each other, grieving for the loss. You can see the suffering on their face and in their posture. They will watch over their relative for days and make mournful-sounding noises, sometimes defending the body against predators."[3]

Crosta mentioned, in particular, the deep pangs felt by elephant mothers at the loss of their babies and the support shown by the rest of the herd. Like Tahlequah, the orca whale mentioned in chapter 6, elephant mothers can be seen carrying their stillborn calves for days as they mourn. And like Tahlequah's pod, the herd refuses to forsake the grieving mother. In a show of support, the other elephants gather in a circle around the mother and allow her the time she needs to grieve. They don't hurry her along or push her to abandon the body. Instead, they gently reach out their trunks and stroke the mother in a show of unwavering support.

I firmly believe that we experience many of our trials not for ourselves but to gain the empathy necessary to help someone else. This entire life is meant to be teamwork—it's an essential part to why we're here! So many of the women I interviewed have learned fulfillment in this life comes as we connect, communicate, and contribute.

Donna

After battling cancer, Donna showed her support to her fellow cancer patients by going to the treatment center and just sitting with people. Donna spoke from experience when she shared, "Sometimes people don't need a big gesture like organizing a giant community fundraiser to help them know you care. Sometimes all you have to do is just be with them. Just let them talk and really listen."

Tracie

Tracie understands firsthand the need for quiet contribution in the wake of a loss. After the death of her father, Tracie felt a bit let down when everyone's lives began going back to normal. People stopped coming by at the same time the shock of her father's death began to wear off and the reality started to sink in. For that reason, Tracie waits until the dust has settled after a loss before going to check on a griever. She told me, "I just feel like everybody goes back to their regular life about two weeks after and that's right when it all becomes 'real.' I like to go visit people when things have quieted down so they know they aren't forgotten. I want them to know they aren't alone, because sometimes when a little time has passed, that's when you need the most support."

Shanette

As a hair dresser, Shanette contributes every day she works by listening to the stories of the women in her salon chair. "You would not believe the things I hear day in and day out," Shanette said with her eyebrows raised high. "But in some ways, it's really neat. I feel like Heavenly Father has given me this opportunity to help others with their problems at the same time as I get to help them do some self-care. They hopefully leave feeling pretty and with a weight off their chest from being able to talk to someone about their problems. It's a win-win."

JoAnne's contribution is studying the gospel deeply and sharing her knowledge, faith, and testimony with others. For Kelsea, it is seeing her son's autism as a gift and giving him opportunities to use it as such. Since Donell has not had the opportunity to be a mother in this life, she instead is a phenomenal, thoughtful friend. Where Cassie had a dysfunctional home in her childhood, she has worked hard to create a safe, loving environment for her children and grandchildren. Marsha, though saddened by her husband's years of substance abuse, seeks to strengthen a positive relationship with him by spending time doing hobbies such as falconry together. After a traumatic miscarriage, Amberlee reaches out to friends if they have a loss and gives them a book that brought her comfort. Julia has known the sting of loneliness and welcomes newcomers with open arms. She is constantly on the lookout for people who may not feel included or accepted so she can offer them attention, friendship and love. These women, and many others, demonstrate the power that small acts can have in creating big change in the world on a one-on-one basis.

Becoming a Contributor might not be seen by the outside world at all. It could be an internal change in your thought processes when you choose to deliberately think optimistically rather than negatively. It might be a change in the way you view people. It might be holding back advice and just listening. The monumental act of you changing the world may be as simple as changing your heart.

Contribution then, in the end, is putting good out into the world that did not exist before. President Gordon B. Hinckley echoed this thought with this call to action: "It's not enough just to be good. You must be good for something. You must contribute good to the world. The world must be a better place for your presence. And the good that is in you must be spread to others. . . . In this world so filled with problems, so constantly threatened by dark and evil challenges, you can and must rise above mediocrity, above indifference. You can become involved and speak with a strong voice for that which is right."[4]

ENDNOTES

1. Neal A. Maxwell, quoted in M. Joseph Brough, "Lift Up Your Head and Rejoice," churchofjesuschrist.org/study/general-conference/2018/10/lift-up-your-head-and-rejoice?lang=eng, October 2018.

2. Rumi, quoted in Tami Shaikh, "Death: The Teacher of Life?" *The Huffington Post*, November 4, 2014, huffpost.com/entry/death-the-teacher-of-life_b_6093364.

3. Elizabeth Edwards, 2007 speech in Cleveland, abcnews.go.com/US/elizabeth-edwards-words/story?id=12337723.

4. Anna Swartz, "Elephant Herd Comforts Grieving Mom Over Loss of Her Calf," thedodo.com/elephant-herd-comforts-grievin-918372088.html.

5. Gordon B. Hinckley, "Stand Up for Truth," speeches.byu.edu/talks/gordon-b-hinckley_stand-truth.

CHAPTER 12

He Will Make Her Wilderness like Eden

"For the Lord shall comfort Zion: he will comfort all her waste places; and he will make her wilderness like Eden, and her desert like the garden of the Lord; joy and gladness shall be found therein, thanksgiving, and the voice of melody."

—Isaiah 51:3

The nurse pushes me in a wheelchair down a hospital hall I have traveled only once before. When she turns toward the first door, my heart skips a beat, then resumes with rapid, anxious palpitations. The unnaturally bright lights of the operating room make me squint as I am wheeled into a sterile space packed tight with equipment and people. The medical team buzzes with activity as they prepare for surgery.

This is the exact room where I delivered my boys three and a half years ago. I heft my enormous pregnant body onto the operating table and practice deep breathing. I tell myself that this time it will be different. This time I will not cradle the still form of my baby, inexplicably waiting to see the rise and fall of his chest, listening for breaths that will never come.

No, today we anticipate smooth sailing as we welcome our final child to our family, our rainbow after the storm. I shut my eyes against the harsh light and pray deeply. "Father, I'm scared. Please calm my heart. Please help me to feel peace. And, Father, if it's possible, please send Aiden to be with me. Wilt thou please let him help me through this?"

The prayer doesn't end. I let it loop on replay as I turn my back to the anesthesiologist, clenching the edge of the table as I round my shoulders inward for clear access to my spine. I resist my instinctual urge to bolt and run. Knowing that stillness is essential, I try to slow the tremors of my body, but the shaking just transfers to my teeth, clattering together uncontrollably like the intense rattling of a car on a road's rumble strip.

Only my obstetrician, remembering my twins, seems to sense my trepidation. He places a gentle hand on my shoulder, and my thoughts instantly flash to Burke waiting anxiously in another room. He should be suited up now and ready to join us for the delivery. I wish he was already here to hold my hand as the rough sound of Velcro being ripped apart jars my already fragile nerves. I am secured to the table as we wait for the spinal to take effect.

And then, everything goes wrong.

The spinal fails to numb me, and I can feel everything. "I can feel that!" I cry out in panic. The team's voices become intense, their words quick and clipped. My head spins as I try to sort out gut-wrenching memories made in this room in the past with the chaotic events of the present. The drugs now pumping in my veins muddle my brain, and my breaths come in short gasps as tears pour from my eyes.

A gas mask is placed over my face and I'm instantly fading. Unconnected thoughts scramble through my brain in one-word bursts. *Baby—Pain—Rainbow—Burke—Where—Afraid—Aiden.*

* * *

I wake to the sensation of a cold wetness soaking me through. My eyes feel weighted down as I attempt to pry them open. It wasn't an illusion; my hospital gown is soaked on my left side from my shoulder to my bottom in some kind of liquid. I make a sound for help. Burke is instantly at my side. "You've got to be kidding me," he says in frustration. My eyes are too heavy and close on their own accord.

Fighting through the fog of my brain, I vaguely process snippets of a conversation Burke has with a nurse. She is embarrassed as she admits someone must have turned the drip line on without actually attaching it to my IV. It's been dripping all right, just *all over* instead of *inside* me. Add it to the mounting list of mistakes made on what was to be a routine C-section.

"Are we surprised?" Burke asks me when I am dry with a fresh gown and sheets. "The anesthesiologist said spinals fail in less than one percent of people." He strokes my hair lovingly and attempts humor. "Of course it would happen to you!"

Throughout the day, as I fade in and out of oblivion for hours at a time, I learn that they suspect I was given the wrong cocktail of drugs to begin with, which has resulted in my failed spinal and an emergency delivery. In a panic, the anesthesiologist had flooded me with an excess of drugs after the spinal had failed. It had been way too much for my small frame, causing my oxygen and heart rates to drop. Whether as a side effect of the wrong medications or simply because my body had responded poorly on its own, as they progressed with the C-section, I had begun to hemorrhage internally. It had taken hours for them to stop the flow of blood. Once I had finally stabilized, they had introduced a new drug after surgery meant to normalize both oxygen levels and heart rates—a drug that was, unfortunately, dripping uselessly on my bed. With so many man-made problems with the delivery, neither Burke nor I had seen the birth of our baby girl, robbing us of that priceless memory forever.

In a haze of medications, I finally meet our precious daughter for the first time. She's healthy and safe, a perfect clone of our other children. We name her Phoebe Erin, meaning Bright Peace.

And yet, as the night closes in and the lights go off, I am suddenly wide awake with feelings that are anything but peaceful. Burke rests in the recliner next to me, Phoebe sleeps deeply in the plastic hospital bassinet beyond, and I try, for a time, to repress the mounting emotions so as not to disturb them.

But then I think of this book. I think of the lessons I have learned from the past three and a half years. I think of the way I have tried to put black ink to white paper in order to sort out my sorrow. I remember the weight of my dirty pain that I am still trying to wash clean. I think of my grief, contained but never gone.

Arlene's wise words from so long ago echo in my mind: "You feel what you need to feel."

So, I do.

And I let go.

I cry out in anguish stemming from the clean pain of missing our boy. I cry in regret for the hole he has left in our family that will never be filled, no matter how much time passes and no matter the immense love that I have for our living children. I cry for the pain the women I have interviewed had to suffer. I cry in gratitude for the resilience they have modeled for me. I cry with relief, thinking how far I have come.

I cry too, in anger, feeling cheated. Why hadn't Aiden been with me in the operating room today? *Couldn't you have spared him for just one day, Father?* I ask in my mind. If there was ever a time when my mother-heart needed him most, it was today.

My weeping wakes Burke and he jumps up. He comes to me, attempting to soothe me, but I won't hide these emotions any longer. I insist on being heard. I pour my heart out to him, speaking aloud all my feelings. I share with him the depth of my sorrow. In that moment of pure vulnerability, I finally—*finally*—relinquish my white-knuckled grip of control and abandon all of my unfounded expectations for myself and my grief.

And as I let go, God is finally able to work His miracles within me. With all my walls crumbled to pieces, He can show me my child.

He is right there beside me. My baby boy, my precious son.

It is as if a window in my mind opens and I am able to see, not with my natural eyes, but with spiritual sight. He looks exactly the way I remember from my glimpse in the hospital the day we learned he had passed. He is in his prime, perhaps twenty, young and strong with his daddy's grin and my eyes. I keep my own eyes shut tight, instinctively knowing that if I open them, the scene will not be the same. However, counterintuitively, I *see* him and the room as clearly as if my eyes were open.

"Oh, Aiden! He's here, Burkie. He's right here."

Aiden rests his hand on mine with a gentle smile. He doesn't say a word, but it's as if I can hear him communicating in my mind, redirecting my thoughts to his sister, fast asleep on the other side of the room. "Phoebe means *peace*, Mom. Her name means peace."

My breathing and tears slow as his message calms me.

I talk out loud. I tell Aiden exactly what has been in my heart over the past several years. My sorrow overflows as I say, "I'm so sorry if it was my fault, Aiden. I'm so sorry if I'm the reason why you weren't able to come."

He smiles and shakes his head. "Mom, you know better."

He stays while he can, no more than one or two sacred minutes. And yet, in that short time, it is as if I can actually feel God's power binding up my wounded heart and making me whole.

I continue to narrate aloud to Burke. Though he cannot see what I do, a near-tangible spirit fills the room, making this space, this moment, sacred beyond words.

Before he leaves, Aiden leans out and reaches his arm across the bed, resting his free hand on Burke's shoulder. With Burke holding my hand on the right and Aiden resting his hand on my left hand, it is as if we are all connected in a perfect triangle of love.

"He's touching your shoulder, Burke," I say out loud. "He says you don't have to be so strong anymore." Tears flood my husband's eyes as he exhales a puff of laughter.

The door to our hospital room opens and he's gone.

In walks a nurse.

"Everything all right in here?" she asks.

I look at my Burkie, who is wiping away tears with the back of his hand, the first I have seen on his face since the day we buried Aiden.

Yes, we are all right. Everything is going to be all right.

"Sisters, I do not know why we have the many trials that we have, but it is my personal feeling that the reward is so great, so eternal and everlasting, so joyful and beyond our understanding that in the day of reward, we may feel to say to our merciful, loving Father, 'Was that all that was required?'"

—Linda S. Reeves,
"Worthy of Our Promised Blessings"

ACKNOWLEDGMENTS

To me, the greatest disappointment of this project was my inability to give adequate time and space to the deeply personal conversations I was blessed to have with these fifty remarkable women. Truly, each woman interviewed deserves an entire book of her own. Although their vignettes are merely a snapshot of their varied life experiences, I am grateful for their courage in allowing me to share brief elements of their lives and wisdom within these pages. The experience of glimpsing the grandeur of their hearts has changed mine irrevocably.

I will forever hold a love for the women of Ministering Moms of Multiples who reached out to me in our hour of darkness. Oh, the unseen power of strangers united in charity! You dear women will never know what your compassionate gestures did for this aching mama's heart.

To my angel mamas on our sister-group, Ministering Moms of *Missing* Multiples, my love and admiration for you continues to grow as I watch you carry your burdens of grief with the grace and perseverance of queens. The way you reach out to and uplift one another inspires me to do more for others.

I am indebted to Jody Moore for her willingness to share her life-changing teachings on thought-work that have *literally* changed my brain. She is an extremely sought-after woman, and yet she was so generous in giving of her time and expertise to answer my questions.

Many thanks are due to the Storymakers community which created space and opportunities for my fledgling author wings to spread. To Jolie Taylor and Ann Rohr who deserve awards for their fantastic edits, and to the team at Cedar Fort Publishing who were so kind, professional, and patient with my numerous questions.

ACKNOWLEDGMENTS

I am full of gratitude to my wonderful support crew of both Bush and Adams family for helping me refine initial manuscripts and encouraging me to carry on whenever my nerve wavered. I am especially grateful for my dad's psychological point of view and input that helped me flesh out elements of grief I may not have considered.

My sweetheart, Burke, has been my constant source of strength and stability throughout the entirety of this challenging, yet rewarding journey. He has encouraged me from day one and deserves an epic ballad for constantly building me up with his tireless optimism as the first and last reader of every page. Each woman interviewed knew upfront that I would maintain the confidentiality of their stories with one exception: every interview would be followed by a decompression session with my Burkie to process the often heavy and heartbreaking revelations and to reflect in admiration on the strength of each brave woman. I could not have borne the weight of their heartaches nor gloried in their strength without him.

And my thanks would not be complete without gratitude expressed to Director of Literary Development, Angie Hodapp, who changed my life at my first writing conference with the four words: "You are a writer."

ABOUT THE AUTHOR

Emily Ann Adams holds a degree in English education and is the creator of Ministering Moms of Missing Multiples, a bereavement support group for mothers who have lost one or more of their multiples. An advocate for exploring the world and embracing diversity, Emily has worked in Mexico teaching English, volunteered with a nonprofit in southern India to help those afflicted with leprosy, and also lived in Paris, France. She and her husband are the parents of four living children and one angel son. *Is There No Other Way: Exploring Growth through Grief* is her debut book and was a winner of the Storymakers First Chapters Writing Contest.